OUTER BANKS
VISIONARIES

OUTER BANKS
VISIONARIES

BUILDING NORTH CAROLINA'S OCEANFRONT

Clark Twiddy

THE
History
PRESS

Published by The History Press
Charleston, SC
www.historypress.com

Copyright © 2023 by Clark Twiddy
All rights reserved

First published 2023

Manufactured in the United States

ISBN 9781467153911

Library of Congress Control Number: 2022951587

Come sit on our porch and let us tell you of the dreams we keep.
—Andy Griffith, on the floor of the North Carolina Legislature, 1982

This book is dedicated to the service of Senator Marc Basnight as an Outer Banks version of Theodore Roosevelt's "Man in the Arena." I hope he would have read it even having lived it.

And to AM and EM and LM, who live it now.

And finally, to those among us who feel that history illuminates the present as much as it does the past.
—CST

CONTENTS

FOREWORD

It's been a privilege for me to spend a big chunk of my banking career here on the Outer Banks during the time this book covers. The kind of banking I've enjoyed, banking at what I believe is banking at its best, is about using the strength of financial markets to help people build things that enrich the lives of others. This is a story of those kinds of markets and those kinds of people. Then, as now, when they intersect well it's a beautiful thing.

For more than thirty years of my life, I've been a participant in the growth of this truly special place and have watched it grow from something relatively small to something relatively astounding in America. I met my wife here, raised a family here and will always call this place home—even as it has changed before my own eyes.

As I try to place in context my journey along these shores, I'm fond of sharing the story of three bricklayers who, when asked what they were doing, had three responses: the first said they were laying bricks. The second said they were building a wall. The third, head down, replied that they were building a cathedral. I love that story because it suggests to me a primacy of purpose over task and the importance of vision over the long term.

This is a book about cathedral builders.

Many of the people in this book I've been fortunate to know as friends, and many of their stories resonate with me as I've been able to see them grow alongside this place. In many ways, the story of the modern Outer Banks is a story of their dreams, their efforts and their friends.

It's also a story of the financial markets that I love. Moving across time, America's financial markets have been the fuel that fired remarkable growth not only nationally but regionally as well. The history of these markets is anything but ordinary—in fact, the shifting sands of financial markets are, if anything, a study of humanity in all its aspects. To imagine, in this day and time, interest rates in the latter stages of Jimmy Carter's presidency in the low 20 percent range is to voyage back to a different time in America. The intervening years have seen a complex story in America and an equally as interesting one along our own shores.

History, as this book points out, illuminates the present as much as it does the past, and to understand where we're going—in banking or in life—we have to first understand how we got where we are today. This is a book about how we got where we are, and it asks questions about where, in turn, we're headed. Success, I've noticed, needs direction. As a result, the future is always just as exciting as it is unknown. While I'm proud to have known so many in this story, I'm equally as convinced that the future lies in yet another generation of cathedral builders that I hopefully have yet to meet.

One thing I know for sure—growth like the kind this place has seen is the story in many ways of my own life, and for that I am grateful. I'm grateful especially for the friendships that helped enrich the lives of so many in their discoveries of the place I have come to love alongside so many. I'm happy to see their story told as it needs to be, lest we forget.

Even though this is a work of history, in the end it also points to the future. Without hesitation, one last thing I know for sure and to quote Dr. Seuss: "Oh the places we'll go!"

—H. Taylor Sugg
President, Towne Bank of Northeastern North Carolina

PROLOGUE

It had been a long time since 1587 and its mysterious Lost Colony, although not much had changed. The U.S. Navy assaulted Roanoke Island during 1862 in an eerie foreshadowing of more famous efforts less than one hundred years later. The Cape Hatteras Lighthouse was lit a few years after the invasion in 1870. The Wright brothers arrived and literally changed the world in 1903 through their vision, and even still the place hadn't changed much since their departure. The lifesaving services and the world wars came and went, too, and left early outlines of what are today several towns meandering along the dune landscapes of the Outer Banks. Famous, yes, if only for its history, but still barren. Finally, road access to the islands came in the early 1930s as a private bridge linked the barrier islands to the rest of the mainland for good. The bridge, built as an investment by wealthy families seeking to develop some of their real estate holdings on the Outer Banks, didn't last long in private hands, and the state eventually took it over. From there, it took one of the greatest statesmen in American history to push forth the future.

The Depression-era election of Franklin Delano Roosevelt in 1932 heralded, among the many points of his campaign, a new approach to relief for Americans reeling from the newly great economic calamity that was straining every aspect of the teetering U.S. economy. In some of the many aspects of his famous New Deal, programs like the Works Progress Administration, the Civilian Conservation Corps and the National Housing

Act of 1934 sought to put Americans to work in a myriad of new roles. In addition, the Roosevelt administration worked to federally carve out significant areas of the American landscape through outright federal ownership and by doing so ensure not only public access to our nation's natural resources but also enough meaningful work to keep hundreds of thousands of people gainfully employed until the free market economy could regain its footing.

In the same year that Roosevelt came to power, about a six-hour car ride to the southeast from Washington in a place that Roosevelt himself would soon visit in the coming decade, the already famous Outer Banks of North Carolina remained in remarkably primitive isolation as the ferocious hurricane of 1933 caused tremendous erosion and the virtual destruction of the community of Portsmouth Island. Roosevelt may have also had a personal connection to the area dating from his earlier days as the assistant secretary of the navy in World War I; the navy secretary at the time, Josephus Daniels, hailed from Eastern North Carolina. Daniels had a son, Jonathan, who was briefly Roosevelt's press secretary in 1940. Roosevelt was to visit the Outer Banks in 1939 and stay, of course, in a vacation home.

More broadly, though, the work relief efforts that Roosevelt envisioned changed the landscape of the Outer Banks in an enduring way. In only one example, various work groups would install more than three million feet of sand fences and countless amounts of beach grass built to stabilize the newly created man-made sand dunes ranging up and down the Outer Banks. To underscore the importance of that stabilization work, Danny Couch, a modern Hatteras businessman, once remarked that it was those dunes that in turn created the oceanfront. That oceanfront, over time, is what brought the change.

Those two forces—the government's increasing work-relief ambition to protect public access through public effort and also the destructive nature of erosion along many of our nation's seashores—began a slow transformation of that moonlike isolation into what is today a globally famous vacation destination featuring billion-dollar visitor economies. Roosevelt laid the foundation stone via his election mandate, and the Outer Banks, as a result, would evolve to a point where an entrepreneurial group of visionaries, years later, could convert his farsighted foundation into a jaw-dropping economy few, if any, could have then imagined.

On this canvas the story now combines a philanthropist and, of course, a visionary real estate man. Henry Phipps, a partner of Andrew Carnegie's

A cyclist looks at beach erosion on NC 12 in Kitty Hawk in 1990s. *Courtesy of the Drew Wilson Outer Banks Collection.*

steel empire and a key developer in places like Miami and Palm Beach, owned over one thousand acres of land as an investment just around the corner from the Cape Hatteras Lighthouse that had been so badly eroded during the 1933 storm. Noted philanthropists, the Phipps family began to think about donating their property to the State of North Carolina as a better alternative than either paying taxes or risking complete erosion. According to the National Park Service, the noted real estate man who helped the Phipps family in that thinking was the painter and outdoorsman Frank Stick, who would go on to be perhaps the pioneering real estate developer of the Outer Banks. In the summer of 1933, Stick published an article in a local Elizabeth City newspaper detailing his dream of a national seashore, titled "A Coastal Park for North Carolina and the Nation."

Over the next several years, various local private interests, elected officials and public staff worked together in ways expressly designed to protect the area while economically developing the region. As a recognition of this vision, Frank Stick was himself appointed by North Carolina's Governor John Ehringhaus (hailing from nearby Elizabeth City) the first chair of an emerging North Carolina Coastal Commission. Over time, Congressman Lindsay Warren, backed by a unique consortium of interests to include local, state and federal support, formally introduced the legislation to create something durable and conservation-minded for the Outer Banks. Warren's secretary, at the time, was a young man—and future congressman—named Herbert C. Bonner.

In 1937, Congress authorized the unique creation of the Cape Hatteras National Seashore as a culmination of a few popular shaping currents—the financial imperative to provide work projects to a burgeoning federal workforce in the form of economic development, a populist political desire to protect public access to America's recreational areas as the nation's seashores increasingly came under wealthy private ownership and a conservationist impulse to preserve vulnerable areas against natural loss due to factors like erosion or pollution. Interestingly, it's worth noting the impulse wasn't to create a boom in the visitor economy. It would take another vision to do that.

The newly created National Seashore was the first of its kind in our nation and appeared in a close timeline with other large-scale federal projects like the Hoover Dam in 1935 and the Blue Ridge Parkway in 1936. In combining conservation and access with public policy, these projects, among many others, set in place an environmental dynamic that continues today as businesses still work alongside the protected public access envisioned in 1937. They remain, in their influence today, almost eerily farsighted; the National Seashore alone in 2021, for example, hosted more than 3.2 million visitors. In addition to the simply stunning visitor commerce dynamic, the federal government remains the largest single landowner in Dare County along the Outer Banks.

While the Seashore itself was authorized in 1937, it took another almost twenty years and the national priority of World War II to assemble the resources and infrastructure needed to meet the federal requirements necessary to open the Seashore to the public, as it didn't open officially until January 1953. By then, the Korean War was concluding, and President Eisenhower ushered in a proverbial deep breath in American domestic policy. The Herbert C. Bonner Bridge, named after Congressman Warren's protégé, was completed ten years later and finally linked Hatteras Island to the rest of the Outer Banks. It was the bridge—and others that followed it—that was the connective tissue to the rest of the world. They were beautiful bridges and beautiful roads.

Broadly, the Seashore opening—the realization of a true public preservation access—was the initial tectonic shift in what would become the Outer Banks's transformation. It would take another burst of torchbearers, from yet another collaboration of public and private interests, to ignite the next flame. Those forces would emerge clearly thirty-three years later in 1986, with a barnstorming band of local entrepreneurs alongside another great statesman from Manteo, North Carolina.

ACKNOWLEDGEMENTS

O f course, there is never enough time or clarity of mind to thank all those who have shaped a story like this. Up front, this book was never intended to be an encyclopedic version of what happened or an academic record of achievement. It is simply my own perspective over time, having seen the boom of our visitor economy stammer and then roar back to life after the bridge reopened in 2020. Importantly, were a journey like this created with judgment of the worthy professionals alongside whom I inhabit my working days, the story would inevitably be much better through their contributions. That said, I am indebted to them for their grace in allowing me to pursue a remote, to some of them, context for our shared modern effort.

Above all, I thank my family—my wife and two girls—for their support in putting up with a man who seems strangely fascinated by so many things lying beyond the moment, tucked away in the dusty-paged minds of those who once lived great lives.

INTRODUCTION

The years teach much that the days never know.
—Emerson

Even since Roosevelt's support of a National Seashore, the Outer Banks had remained sleepy in its villages as summer breezes lifted any ambition of its residents or occasional visitors. World War II saw a migration of much of the small local workforce to various war efforts. A good portion of that population was never to return, as jobs off the island—particularly in nearby Norfolk, Virginia—became more attractive than the scarce jobs on the islands. The decades of the 1950s, '60s and '70s saw a quiet Outer Banks not too distinct from the views of Orville and Wilbur Wright—isolated jeep-tracked dunes, remote stretches of barren beaches and smatterings of know-all-your-neighbor towns and villages among the seascapes of the ocean. During that period, Aycock Brown, that first marketer of the Outer Banks and for whom the Kitty Hawk Visitor Center is named, worked tirelessly in his efforts to promote the Outer Banks as a summer destination through his popular photography and strong advertising relationships. Sarah Owens, for whom the Manteo Visitor Center is named, kept these small tourism efforts running amid Brown's creativity. These two remarkable individuals were the lighthouses, in a sense, for what would become a sunrise of interest.

For many years, in fact, the Outer Banks was known to many people as simply Nags Head or even Manteo (the road sign for the Outer Banks in nearby Chesapeake, Virginia, up until 1994 said simply "Nags Head").

Outer Banks pre-development aerial. *Outer Banks History Center.*

The Outer Banks Chamber of Commerce, for example, started as the Nags Head Chamber of Commerce and spent much of its life that way. It was Brown who saw a greater vision for a more regional destination made up of a collection of places—Ocracoke, Hatteras, Kitty Hawk and north to even the sandy duck hunting grounds of Corolla. It was the Outer Banks as a place that first emerged from Brown's photographic lens, and the Outer Banks as a term probably didn't really catch on in the popular memory until Jim Douglas and Dave Wallace coined the abbreviation "OBX" in 1994—but that was all in the future as the mid-1980s came into view.

For reasons we will begin to uncover, the 1980s saw a different tide begin to arrive, and it is here that our story truly begins. This decade marked an inflection point for the entire region, and the beach's economic current was simply never again the same. Looking to the future as a place, it's important to understand—or at least place in context—not only the architecture of how this place so rapidly grew but also why and how it did so in a way that remains nearly unique in the nation. Of course, embedded within these contexts are the seeds of the future.

Above: Risky real estate and development ventures prompted Pioneer Savings Bank to close its Nags Head, North Carolina branch doors in 1991. *Outer Banks History Center.*

Left: An early Outer Banks real estate company. *Outer Banks History Center.*

The key elements in that transformation began as a fortunate intersection between four things: first, an entrepreneurial collection of like-minded risk-takers; second, the turbulent capital and commerce markets that funded them largely in the Reagan era; third, the political will and subsequent infrastructure investments that made the movement of commerce and capital accessible; and finally, the relatively affordable Outer Banks development canvas that was just raw enough to be wholly shaped while being just sturdy enough to sustain the change. It was enough to delight any entrepreneurial mind—to this day, few are the conversations among visitors that don't begin with a personal discovery date of when someone started coming to the Outer Banks. The times had that kind of hold on the imagination, and those early beachgoers wanted, simply, to share in the place. In the same way that the moon landing marked a memorable moment for a nation, so too did the first few blinks of the Outer Banks in its still original form. It was a moment, peering over the dunes toward the ocean, seldom forgotten in the eyes of the beholders.

More nationally, the larger year of 1986 stands out in most of our memories as the year of the Challenger disaster, most likely, or the unforgettable Iran-Contra testimony that riveted much of the nation as President Reagan's landslide second term began. The nuclear calamity of Chernobyl sticks out as the initial domino in the Soviet-ending perestroika, as does a sense of financial relief from the shocks of the late 1970s. Among financial minds, the first public offering of the vaunted House of Morgan's financial stock arrived, as well as the launch of the consumer-friendly Apple II computer with the internet—that changer of all things—being born just three years earlier. KKR had done the first leveraged buyout only seven years before in 1979, and North Carolina's famous "barbarians at the gate" drama transpired in the mid-1980s.

By 1986, the recession of 1980 had fully cleared, and financial assets in both traditional banks and also mortgage-minded savings-and-loan entities were on a pronounced rebound. Financial stocks soared for much of the year, and critically, interest rates retreated to a decade low following both regulatory and policy guidance designed to stimulate growth as an antidote to the so-called stagflation of the early 1980s. Tax reform was enacted with broad support, and for much of main street America, a smooth economic boom flowed toward the last decade of the twentieth century.

In short, with the increase in banking assets and the decrease in interest rates, home purchases in the United States began to increase. Nationally, median home prices, for example, in 1980 were $62,500 and only ten years later had doubled to $125,000. While the Outer Banks remained largely remote, it was also increasingly near major population centers that boomed during the Reagan years—the massive Northern Virginia defense industrial complex, the major Norfolk naval and commercial footprints and the financial institutions around them all flourished through the middle of the decade. As they did so, many of the participants in that financial boom began to think about a second home as a result of their new affluence and found that banks would be willing to loan them the money to build it. In the language of business, that falling-rate and rising-market dynamic unleashed a private equity boom in for-sale residential markets across the country, and the Outer Banks, once again, was discovered.

As these homebuyers evolved in their search, they turned with their curiosity to their friends who had visited the Outer Banks themselves, perhaps on a hunting or fishing trip (Frank Stick's first trip was a fishing expedition). Maybe they even saw a smattering of newspaper advertisements, placed by farsighted Outer Banks business owners, advertising a beautiful family-friendly destination that was truly affordable. The question, they asked their friends, was did they meet anyone who might know about real estate? Or equally as possible, their friends had just purchased a lot—maybe even a simple home—and were enjoying the remoteness of the place as if they were a member of a secret club. In turn, and as with all secrets, they were happy to make an introduction and share their secret. That's where the story really begins and where an industry was born.

1

THE CHANGING CHEMISTRY
OF COMMERCE

As this is written, little fear is visible on Wall Street.
—Warren Buffet in his annual letter, 1986

THE SULLEN SEEDS OF 1981

It is a crisis that strikes at the very heart and soul of our national will.
We can see this crisis in the growing doubt of the meaning of our own
lives and in the loss of unity and purpose as a nation. The erosion of
confidence in the future is threatening to destroy the social and political
fabric of the nation.
—Jimmy Carter, addressing what he perceived to be a national crisis of
confidence, 1979

To fully understand the economic environment of the mid-1980s that fueled the visions of those Outer Banks entrepreneurs before they are introduced, some economic context is in order so as to best understand their decision-making landscape. The best place to start might be the national economic environment that was emerging from the second half of Jimmy Carter's presidential term from 1979 to 1981. If we can understand the transitioning financial equilibrium from 1981 to 1986, we can understand the minds of those who signed their names to the loan documents that changed the Outer Banks.

Nationally, the economy lagged for about eleven years between the end of LBJ's term in 1968 and 1979, and with Jimmy Carter's election in 1978, a pivotal point had been reached. It was Carter's luck to make the tough decisions to pivot the national economy from a period of stagflation to a period of economic growth. Those decisions—both within his administration and in the minds of American voters—are the first act in the play.

Jimmy Carter's busy administration was combating double-digit inflation and historically high interest rates, fresh off a worrisome energy crisis in a nation still reeling from Vietnam and Watergate. Given the challenges of today's stagflationary economy, it can be tough to fully understand the challenging dynamics of those years. To frame the issue clearly, the transition between the Carter years and the Reagan years was to see a shift from a stagflating run beginning in 1968 and running through 1981 to a generally pronounced forty-year era of falling interest rates and rising equity markets.

Interest rates soared in the late 1970s and quickly became the highest in United States history—ten-year treasuries, in late 1981, reached 15.8 percent, and some prime interest rates settled in the 21.5 percent range (and higher depending on credit). The economy broadly and financial markets in particular were historically depressed. Worse still, borrowers and lenders alike knew that the inevitable cure—keeping rates high for longer—only kept the economy slow in the short term. The other alternative was a presidential election the following year and a change of course.

Subsequent and crippling short-term stagflation through 1981 was one of the prime reasons that Jimmy Carter, a wartime navy veteran and recent successful governor of Georgia, become the first incumbent U.S. president since Herbert Hoover in 1932 (in the wake of another economic calamity; Hoover subsequently lost to Franklin Roosevelt) to not be reelected to a second term.

While in office, though, Carter worked to stabilize the economy. One personnel move—perhaps his signature presidential appointment—that would affect credit markets right away was Carter's decision to appoint Paul Volcker in 1979 to head the Federal Reserve, with the nudging of Wall Street financial interests, as a gesture toward combating rapidly increasing inflation. To Carter's unending credit, his political courage in making the tough decision to appoint someone who would force through a painful economic approach that would win few friends in the short-term remains admirable. Volcker would, in turn, solve the crisis for another president.

The towering Volcker had been the head of the powerful New York Fed at the time of his appointment and had a long track record both on Wall Street and in government, specifically within the Treasury Department. Volcker's policies, soon to become known as the "Volcker Shock," are what led to intentionally staggering interest rate increases in an effort to rapidly shrink the monetary supply and by extension choke off the consuming fire of inflation. While painful, the approach is widely considered to have worked but not in time to save Carter's presidency. Volcker himself, however, would be reappointed to a second term as the Federal Reserve chair in 1983 and would be succeeded by Alan Greenspan in 1987.

With the presidential election of Ronald Reagan in 1981 shaping a new economic mandate, a sharp and inevitable recession moved quickly as markets absorbed the shocks of monetary policy through a presidential transition. Volcker's plan was working, in short, and the credit markets as well as the larger economy fueled by them began to improve. It would take a subsequent second term, however, for Reagan's signature approach to economic policy to really take off.

AN OPTIMISTIC 1986

It's morning again in America. Today more men and women will go to work than ever before in our country's history. With interest rates at about half the record highs of 1980, nearly 2,000 families today will buy new homes, more than at any time in the past four years. This afternoon 6,500 young men and women will be married, and with inflation at less than half of what it was just four years ago, they can look forward with confidence to the future.
—*Ronald Reagan's "Morning in America" ad, 1984*

After Ronald Reagan's pronounced second presidential election victory in 1986, the mandate for his so-called Reaganomics policy of growth-oriented tax reduction, Cold War military spending, market deregulation as a reflection of globalization and stability-minded slower monetary growth seemed poised to continue in full effect. The stock markets reacted positively to this with Dow Jones equity growth in both 1985 and 1986 eclipsing 20 percent. The key financial priority of his second term, the Tax Reform Act, slashed federal income tax rates (and by extension raised discretionary spending) and the overall number of tax brackets, reducing some personal tax rates from 50 percent to 28 percent and keeping home mortgage interest tax deductible while removing deductions for other kinds of personal spending (such as credit card debt, for example).

Mortgage rates, which began the 1980s at a high point of 18.4 percent on average in October 1981, had by 1986 been *cut in half* to the 9 percent range in 1986 (down from that historic 21.5 percent number in less than a decade). Inflation, as a reflection of slowing monetary supply growth, was moderating, meaning purchasing power was increasing (for example, Walmart reported a 32 percent gain in sales in 1986 alone). Home starts and home sales were up, and the first modern interconnected economic crisis of 1987 seemed like a long way off—Black Monday, as it is known, featured a 22 percent loss that remains the largest single-day stock market decline in history. While 1987 is remembered for that day, it's also useful to point out for our understanding that prior to that, the Dow Jones Industrial Average had been up 44 percent that year alone, on top of double-digit gains in prior years.

As a practical matter along the Outer Banks, these national shifts essentially fueled two things: the first was cheaper capital, as falling rates lowered interest expenses and by extension increased returns to equity on the supply side of vacation homes. Second, on the demand side, the growing national economy created more disposable income in places that benefited from the Reagan-era defense boom—namely, core Outer Banks markets in places like Washington, D.C., Philadelphia and the mid-Atlantic corridor. That growing income created in part a growing trend for visitors to the area.

Even with relatively bright economic trends making the Outer Banks more attractive, there were also subtle banking (and credit market) trends that were changing the environment for lending. Interstate banking, something that prior to 1985 had been problematic at the regulatory level, began to change in 1985. The Douglas Amendment to the Bank Holding Company Act essentially began to allow the states themselves to consider whether out-of-state banks should be allowed to buy other state-chartered banks (this deregulatory impulse is linked to Reagan's focus on market deregulation). This led, in turn, to the Riegle-Neal Act of 1994, which gave banks much more freedom to grow nationally and paved the way for national banks at large. Along the Outer Banks during that time, for example, the long-standing Planters Bank merged with Peoples Bank to become Centura. In turn, Centura was acquired by the Royal Bank of Canada to become RBC Centura in 2001, which later became the nationally oriented Pittsburgh National Bank (more commonly known as PNC) in 2012.

At the local level, those overall growth conditions leading up to increasing deregulation and the 1987 crash had made it, in short, easier to lend money to home buyers and builders. In search of market share, banks increasingly competed for customers by aggressively lowering rates as rates fell. That competition ultimately brought value to customers through cheaper borrowing costs. Critically, the savings-and-loan industry locally was able to make even more risky loans reflecting their relatively unique structures (although they wouldn't last much longer as a reflection of that risk).

All told, the capital and credit markets during that time were remarkably favorable by historical comparison to local builders and dreamers in context to the recent Carter years. The ability to access capital is always a competitive advantage for business growth—now, that availability of capital could be linked to those who would be willing to take risks in using it. But before we get to those entrepreneurs, it's worth also pausing for a moment to understand the difference locally between a bank and a savings-and-loan world. Banks, classically, take deposits and in turn make loans. They're regulated, transparent and insured up to a point by the federal government (via an act going back to Roosevelt's election). Borrowers in 1986 had a choice, though, to use loans from multiple sources, and those choices are worth a pause in our understanding.

COMPETITION AMONG LEADING BANKS AND SAVINGS-AND-LOAN MODELS

Any discussion of home buying in the mid-1980s is incomplete without at least a brief mention of the savings-and-loan industry. In short, the savings-and-loan financial basis was linked to the policy desire for private homeownership going back many decades. Over time, the industry became increasingly vulnerable to fluctuations in interest rates (recall the interest rate environment during that time) and in many cases developed long-term debt structures that simply weren't serviceable with lower interest rates funded in the short term. As a result, the industry—aided by supportive regulatory environments that in effect incentivized risky lending—increasingly relied on riskier lending to provide better returns to meet long-term obligations. The analogy at hand is the gambler who, in order to recover early small bets, wagers ever higher amounts in an effort to merely break even from those early bets. As that dynamic grew increasingly risky, the system itself was overwhelmed and famously collapsed.

Locally, the savings-and-loan industry was active in the lending markets around the construction of rental home communities. Many of their loans were considered remarkably aggressive compared to local banks, although the lending environment overall was considered favorable to many would-be buyers and builders—one local storyteller clearly remembers envelopes of cash that arrived as the fulfillment of a loan application. Of course, the music stopped for the local savings-and-loan providers as the larger system supporting the loan concept collapsed under its own weight, peaking in 1988. Today, there remain a few local buildings dotting the main roads that were once home to the now-gone savings-and-loan providers, although they are of course flagged under different names—to the historian, those buildings provide a visual reminder of risks during the boom years.

RELATIVE AFFORDABILITY ALONG THE COAST— DOLLARS THAT WENT FURTHER

With the context of the national economy fresh in the mind, thinking back to the chemistry of commerce relative to our understanding of growth, it's important to consider the key ingredients in what sustained the vacation home growth dynamic of the Outer Banks during that time. In addition to the availability of capital at rates that were heavily discounted from recent levels, one additional key facet in that dynamic was the overall affordability of real estate compared to many destinations across the mid-Atlantic coastal region. Lots in many subdivisions were relatively cheap in comparison to lots in more commonly known areas such as Virginia Beach, Ocean City or Rehoboth Beach. With aggressive lending options, the chances to buy a lot and build a home became much more accessible to a public that for many years had simply been priced out of much of the oceanfront market. Doug Twiddy, another noted local entrepreneur, put it this way:

The Outer Banks has always been a blue-collar beach, and there's a reason for that—we were affordable at the time. Once we had that, we found that families would come back every year and start their own traditions. Once we discovered that, we began to get a sense of what these new rental homes might rent for over the course of a year, and once we had a sense of that we

A 1990 aerial of Whalebone Junction, an area within Nags Head, North Carolina, where three major highways converge (US 64, US Route 158, NC 12). *Outer Banks History Center.*

knew we had a business over time. The big homes may get the headlines, but blue-collar repeat visitors are who brought us to the dance.

As with many of the early business builders, the beginnings of the boom came not in large-scale visitors but in the burgeoning sales of lots and homes to give them a place to stay. This dynamic is difficult to underestimate—for example, lots in Duck were during that time much cheaper than similar lots in Nags Head. A buyer might have looked at a lot in Nags Head for $35,000 and a similar lot in Duck for $21,000. Over time, that dynamic moved north to Corolla as well, as newly accessible tracts presented as bigger and more affordable to other areas. In short, many of the developing areas of the Outer Banks were available at cheaper prices but similar if not better quality than the more established oceanfront areas of Nags Head.

It's important to note in that affordability equation a feature about the limited road network on the Outer Banks. The Nags Head, Kill Devil Hills and Kitty Hawk areas had two roads—the oceanside beach road, as it was known locally, and then the larger bypass road through the middle of the island. Oceanfront lots in this area all backed up to the beach road. That was not the case in the Duck and northern beaches, though—once visitors turned left at the primary intersection in Kitty Hawk, there was only one road. It was soundside in its course, away from the ocean, and that road layout meant that there was more space along the ocean to develop for

Vintage sign for Ocean Dunes, an oceanside community located in Duck, North Carolina. *Courtesy of Twiddy & Company.*

private use. Oceanfront lots from Duck north did not have a road backing up to them, and that fact wasn't lost on those entrepreneurs—in effect, there was more good real estate and at a lower cost to the buyer. In addition, that road layout also meant that many of the planned communities of the Outer Banks were built north of Kitty Hawk as a function purely of space because there was no oceanside road to get in the way of a homesite. In an interesting piece of historic irony, it was our noted real estate man from the Roosevelt years, Frank Stick, who would go on to build, in 1947, the first planned community on the Outer Banks in the town of Southern Shores just to the north of the two-road sections of the Outer Banks.

Over time, that trend continued—many buyers, having discovered Duck, would look for more space and continue north to areas around Corolla. Buyers in Corolla, in search of ever more space, would continue north to the still-unpaved areas in Swan Beach and Carova. That trend—Duck, then Corolla and then the northern beaches—was very much born in the late 1980s as well. Of note, it's that section of the Outer Banks that today has many of the finest homes, highest annual rental rates and a sense of exclusivity that is the envy of many vacation markets across the southeastern United States.

WORKING MARKETS THAT COMBINED SUPPLY AND DEMAND—THE THINGS THEY BUILT

As we continue, it may be useful to point out for a moment the business models that were taking place in these new communities and investments. Broadly, the Outer Banks was to become famous for, among other things, a nationally watched vacation rental market that brought together three previously disparate groups:

HOMEOWNERS, willing to take a long-term asset risk on a home that they can rent for income and also use for their own utility. In renting the home, owners generate revenue to offset the costs of ownership and hopefully in the end own a home with help in paying for it.

THEIR GUESTS, who pay in the short term for the chance to use that home as their own, but without the operating costs or long-term asset risk. Over time, most homeowners have been guests first and figured out the business from there. The probability of those guests to return, year after year and market cycle after market cycle, is a foundational trend to the growth of the Outer Banks.

PROPERTY MANAGERS AND SERVICE PROVIDERS, who combine marketing and services to create both confidence for non-resident homeowners and a consistently good experience for their guests.

It was the early developers who, as they planned oceanside communities, sensed a change in the second home dynamic; for many years, the few Outer Banks second homes had been for the exclusive use of relatively wealthy families in summer months. Their entrepreneurial insight was that, in support of larger-scale affordability, they might be able to market these newer homes to potential guests who would in turn, through their rental income, make the affordability of a beach home much more achievable. This business model—in which a rental home became an operating company that sought to generate more revenue than cost—was an inflection point as well. Combine the consistency of a revenue stream with access to capital and a growing potential market, and we see an equation that changes the tide of a beautifully remote stretch of beach.

In summary, the contexts of a credit market hungry for investment, a local geography that was a virtually blank canvas and emerging business models all came into close contact in the mid-1980s. We now turn, in our understanding, to the bold dreamers who forcefully grabbed those dynamics and wrought them, like iron, into what would become an ironclad economy.

A family in Duck walks by sailboats on Currituck Sound in 1990s. *Courtesy of the Drew Wilson Outer Banks Collection.*

A GEOGRAPHY THAT REMAINS UNIQUE

One of the reasons the Outer Banks as a place is unique is pure geography—as the area is a collection of sandy barrier islands, it is accessible by only two main bridges. For the northern Outer Banks—the area from Nags Head north to the Virginia line—access is via a bridge from the Currituck mainland. In an interesting geographical facet, the Currituck Outer Banks is only accessible from the south and only via Dare County. From the north, the federal government controversially prohibits any kind of vehicular access to the Outer Banks, even going so far as to erect a fence in 2002 (it remains one of the few places in the United States where fences prohibit free travel from state to state). In effect, when roads finally came north from Duck in the late 1970s and early 1980s, Corolla was literally at the end of the line—remote, barren, undeveloped and in many ways untouched. That remoteness enhanced several of the development characteristics we will uncover as we begin to meet the dreamers who, upon sensing a change in the economic wind, were delighted.

2

THE COURAGE TO SEE THROUGH
THE WAVES

The Improbable Market Makers

Dreamers dream about things being different.
Visionaries envision themselves making a difference.
—*Andy Stanley*

LIGHTNING ALONG THE TIDE

Socrates teaches to always begin with a definition. The word *entrepreneur*, for example, has quite a few definitions that have changed over time, but there is some consensus around the notion that an entrepreneur is a focused organization-builder willing to accept larger risks to build greater things in many cases because they simply love what they are doing. What made the Outer Banks landscape unique in this regard is that the small collection of business-minded residents on the beach during that time were indeed entrepreneurial in the classic sense but also had an opportunity to shape not only both their organizations in their infancy but also the visitor economies in which they grew. They could, in other words, build their businesses as well as their market environments—this entrepreneurial compounding was the masterclass in their success. Generations of entrepreneurs in more mature industries had been trained that while one could not control the market environment, they could control the decisions they made in it. This Outer Banks dynamic of both organization and business environment flew in the face of much of that traditional thinking. This notion intuitively makes sense—as we meet these early entrepreneurs, it's clear that, as with so many entrepreneurs, they are mavericks in the face of conventional wisdom.

Outer Banks pre-development aerial. *Outer Banks History Center.*

As these businessmen launched their visions, we'll see that over time, many of the larger local organizations that exist today began as smaller firms focused on specific communities that they could shape relative to development, marketing and service delivery. Few, if any, local organizations started as an overall destination provider—that kind of scale and scope was yet to come, and when it did it was as they had built it.

It was that distinct dual opportunity that marked something unique at that moment when combined with the national and business dynamics mentioned earlier—the shared recognition among a few local visionaries that an opportunity had emerged combined with their own willingness to exploit it through their talents and creativity. If that idea could be constructed with friendly capital and made accessible through roads, they said on their porches over oysters and bourbon, the Outer Banks could bust wide open. As an analogy to the wildcatters of West Texas from an earlier time, they wondered if they had hit a gusher. Never in their wildest dreams, they would learn, could they see just how much they had or how the road before them would twist and turn along the way.

RICHARD "DICK" BRINDLEY
AND A VISION FOR COROLLA

Duck, North Carolina, in 1978 was anything but a destination. You couldn't really even get lost there, as it had only one road in and out—you knew it and perhaps turned around ahead of time. A few folks lived there and fewer than that worked there, but for the most part, it was an almost forgotten stretch of windy salt marshes and desolate sand beaches. During World War II, it was used as a bombing range by fliers from the nearby military airfields of Virginia.

It surely hadn't begun to be considered by millions of travelers as a remarkable place to vacation.

More than thirty years later, Duck and its neighbor to the north, Corolla, stand as some of the most pristine and exclusive vacation destinations in the United States. Every year, the inhabitants of these towns welcome millions of visitors to enjoy the truly unique natural environment and the still-authentic sense of a family memory in a place like no other.

Our story, then, turns from those millions of visitors to the mere handfuls of dreamers who could see it before anyone else. The inevitable question, in turn, becomes—who were these people, and how did they see it so clearly?

Dick Brindley was a giant of a man, ever-smiling and retired once already from the phone company. A West Virginia University alum, his seemingly crazy idea to develop a barren stretch of remote beach along North Carolina's northeastern Corolla corner as a premier vacation home destination came across to many as confounding, although his idea had worked once before just to the south in Duck but at a much smaller scale in a community called Northpoint. Northpoint was a planned home community just to the north of the village of Duck, built as roads and utilities improved and designed for weekly vacation rentals starting along the ocean and working back toward the sound. This trend, starting first at the ocean and working back toward the sound, was indeed a reversal from the old duck club approach that had been among the first kinds of economic development along the beaches about one hundred years earlier, as the early duck clubs (the Whalehead Club in Corolla being a prime example) were inevitably focused on the soundside first. Northpoint was ocean-focused, though, and it shocked many by having an indoor pool closer to the road as an amenity.

Brindley successfully built the Northpoint community, learned from it and had fun doing it, and then, as many others did, he turned his eye north to the still larger undeveloped tracts in Corolla. It was 1986,

A long-haul seine crew works in Pamlico Sound in the late 1980s. *Courtesy of the Drew Wilson Outer Banks Collection.*

Corolla's Historic Whalehead Club at sunset. *Courtesy of Twiddy & Company.*

and large tracts just to the north were becoming available for purchase. Brindley, in a time before things like initial public offerings became popular, was about to take the idea of private stay in a private beach home to the masses, and as it turns out, they loved it. It was ten years before the phrase Vrbo was born with a one-home offering in Colorado via the internet. Nationally, a tiny trade group called the Vacation Rental Managers Association was founded. Brindley was well ahead of them all.

Just to the north of Duck, the tiny village of Corolla had long been known as a popular hunting and fishing area. Hunting clubs like the famous Whalehead Club or the Pine Island Club owned vast swaths of ocean-to-sound real estate, often bought years earlier for astoundingly low amounts. (The Currituck Shooting Club, for example, bought 3,100 acres of land in 1857 for a dollar an acre.) As the ages and stages of the hunt club owners and the sport itself began to change, they began to sell some of their holdings with an eye to making money from rising values. In short, tracts of land started to become available, as opposed to just lots, and those tracts held an equally vast potential for development. Many of the modern communities of the northern Outer Banks were born from duck club holdings, and those tracts got Brindley's attention.

An Outer Banks sunrise. *Courtesy of Twiddy & Company.*

Like Disney World or Las Vegas, the initial ideas around what is today the glittering Corolla Light Resort rode alongside the gleeful Brindley in a bulldozer's seat with a small handful of slightly entertained and disbelievingly optimistic local partners standing alongside his path. His vision, it turns out, for an amenity-heavy resort community in the tiny fishing village of Corolla fired in part the engines of a public attraction to the Outer Banks that resonates across much of the United States today. The small investments of a few of Brindley's friends were among the first of many billions of dollars in private investment that launched, in a year famous for launches, an inflection point in the history of tourism in North Carolina and along the Eastern Seaboard. He was that kind of man.

Brindley convinced a small group of investors to help him buy 240 acres of ocean-to-sound land for the then-princely sum of just over $3 million. At the end of the long, curvy and singular road north from Duck, he was fresh off his lessons learned from what worked in his first community and was excited to begin again on a grander scale. For many years, large-scale private landowners in the Corolla area had preserved the area as private property, even maintaining a manned guard gate at the entrance along the only road to Currituck County from Dare County. In 1984, that guard gate came down as the landowners themselves began to think

An early Twiddy & Company office. *Courtesy of Twiddy & Company.*

about development. It was, for the area of the Currituck Outer Banks, a seminal moment.

Brindley's Corolla Light idea took everything he learned from the Northpoint community and went even further as Corolla became accessible. Good friend and longtime business associate Doug Twiddy shared this anecdote:

> *Dick and I flew into Jacksonville, Florida, and then drove up the coast together looking at many of the fine oceanfront communities along the way back up to Corolla. I remember that Kiawah Island had an oceanfront pool and so did a few others. We knew then that we had to have one, too. And Dick, sure enough, put one in. His Northpoint community had the pool much further back off the ocean, but he figured out that the oceanfront pool would do a better job of attracting families. And it did. And it still does.*

A wild horse grazes on the beach. *Courtesy of Twiddy & Company.*

Some of the early Duck buyers became, in turn, some of the earliest buyers along the ocean in Corolla Light. Notably, Corolla Light was intentionally designed from the ground up to be a vacation rental community attracting families and friends to the beautiful and uncrowded beaches of Corolla. The oceanfront pool complex had a restaurant, and grand parks and recreational facilities dotted the landscape of the resort. There was commercial space at the entrance and even a large recreation center on the west side of the highway with a massive indoor pool and fitness center (fittingly, it bears Brindley's name). The resort has trolley service, an extensive walking trail network and a wide array of common areas. It was, to say the least, ahead of its time.

Today, the resort is virtually inseparable from Corolla, and Corolla is in turn inseparable from the Currituck Outer Banks. With the successful additions of both Northpoint and then Corolla Light, Brindley's legacy on the Outer Banks would be the vision, design and development of planned vacation home communities. They would be the first of many in the area, all jostling to compete with growing numbers of visitors.

To put the increase Brindley sparked in perspective, visitors to the Corolla area, in the subsequent years between 1986 and 1996, grew from about 4,200 people a week in 1986 to about 20,000 a week by the end of 1996.

Families enjoy time at the beach during the '80s. *Courtesy of Twiddy & Company.*

In turn, the full-time population of the Corolla area grew during that same period from about 170 people to 620 residents—a 262 percent increase based largely on the newly created job engine of vacation homes. In terms of homes, there were about 70 homes in the area with full-time residents; by 1996, that number had grown to 255. Brindley had, in fact, changed the place fundamentally and forever.

BOB OAKES AND THE VILLAGE AT NAGS HEAD

At the same time Brindley was building the Corolla Light community, another noted Outer Banks real estate developer was at work building a rental market in the more widely known Nags Head area. In 1986, Bob Oakes began working for a company called Capital Dominion. In conjunction with a few other investors, he began to build out a collection of amenity-rich vacation rental homes in a signature amenity-and-golf community called the Village at Nags Head. Not unlike Corolla Light, this community had an oceanfront pool and also envisioned a "westside" golf community in addition to its oceanside home focus. This community, distinctly different from the more traditional "unpainted aristocracy" of the single-family and private vacation homes just over the sand dunes, was a second and nearly simultaneous development that changed the dynamic on the Outer Banks. In conjunction with the Corolla Light arrival, the Village of Nags Head became a model foundation for the new development approach on the Outer Banks.

Described in a University of Virginia alumni magazine as the "Mayor of Summertime," Oakes went on to build an accompanying service company in Village Realty and serve in a wide array of governmental and advocacy organizations to include long stints leading Nags Head as mayor and commissioner. Going back to our earlier thought around unique entrepreneurial opportunities to shape not only businesses but environments as well, Oakes's public service made him a pivotal figure in the growth of Nags Head as a public and scalable destination.

Notably, his courageous vision for beach nourishment in Nags Head was well ahead of its time and was the first local example of what would become a state- and countywide investment for beach stabilization to support the visitor economy—the first of its kind since the 1930s. Controversial at the time because of its cost and reasoning, the nourishment approach is today widely regarded as a needed and appropriate investment in the visitor

Bonnett Street beach access. *Courtesy of Twiddy & Company.*

economy that singularly sustains the region. Dare County alone, for example, has spent hundreds of millions of dollars on ongoing nourishment projects with state and federal support.

Combined with the development push to the north, the combined efforts of Brindley and Oakes would become the anchor-holds of the prime visitor economy of the Outer Banks for decades to come. North Carolina Highway 12 would be officially extended north to Corolla in 1987, for example, and road improvements would continue through the 1980s and 1990s.

JIM BRAITHWAITE: THE GOVERNOR OF DUCK, NORTH CAROLINA AND THE DEVELOPMENT "ROSETTA STONE"

In between Corolla to the north and Nags Head to the south, the small village of Duck was just beginning to come to life as well. Historically a small community on the northern side of Dare County, the Duck area was identified as a "beautification project" by the North Carolina legislature in 1984 in an act, essentially, that funded via a levied tax the installation of underground, versus overhead, power lines. That kept views and vistas intact—something that made Duck different from other communities on the Outer Banks. A few years later, Duck also received grant funding from Dare County and assistance from the State Board of Transportation to begin to adopt multiuse trails that would begin to define the community in the years to come.

Longtime local property owner and businessman Jim Braithwaite lived in Duck during the time—in between Brindley's Corolla vision and Oakes's work in Nags Head—and remembers seeing it beginning to change:

> *I felt like it didn't really take off until the 1990s, but clearly the seeds and some of the early risks were there in the eighties as well. Duck saw a convenience store open in the early 1980s (Jerry Davis opened a store called Winks in Duck as an extension of their main store in Kitty Hawk), and as folks looked at that and saw it flourishing, other people came along. Walter Story took a big risk and built a big shopping center (Scarborough Faire) in Duck in 1983, and then we built our collection of waterfront shops in 1985.*

Braithwaite also noticed another interesting facet of the economy:

> For so long we had just simple beach houses—no pools and nothing fancy at all. During that time, it was still tough to make a living in the area because those homes, once they were built, didn't need much when people weren't there. Over time, though, amenities started to get bigger. Things like pools and landscaping needed maintenance, and it was those home maintenance jobs that really started to support a full-time visitor economy.

In Braithewaite's mind, Brindley and Oakes had cracked an ecosystem code in a way—they sensed that in addition to simple homes, these communities would also have high levels of amenities, and that's what would make them different. In turn, that's what would make them financially viable for homeowners, and the demands to maintain those amenities would employ countless service professionals in the years to come. It was that changing dynamic that really started to employ people beyond the traditional jobs of the government or commercial fishing. Once that employment engine started to pick up in 1986, yet another inflection point had been reached. With rental homes came jobs—full time and vibrant. That was one of the biggest changes of all.

Braithwaite concluded by adding:

> I went to Home Depot the other day. For starters, we didn't have anything like that until rental communities came along. Anyway, I used to know all the plumbers and all the electricians. Every single one. Now, in the Home Depot parking lot, I don't know anyone, but the lot is full of ladder racks and service providers to rental homes. Those big amenities changed the Outer Banks forever.

Together, visions like that of Oakes and Braithwaite helped change Dare County in many of the same ways Brindley's efforts did in Corolla. Dare County's full-time population, from 1985 to 1995, grew 48 percent as people returned to follow a growing job market. Commercial construction over that time grew at 276 percent in terms of value. Dare County's housing network, made up of a census-reported 11,000 homes in 1980, ended 1990 with 21,567—a 96 percent increase in a decade. Critically and most tellingly, the Saturday "check-in" visitor traffic over the bridges more than doubled during that same time. Currituck and Dare Counties had turned the page, and the torches lighting the path over the next several decades had been lit.

Of note, this developer/property manager/service provider commerce dynamic carried with it great operating potential over the long term. Curiously, in most cases, the actual developers were not the rental home managers and vice versa. When done well, as in the Corolla Light and Village at Nags Head, the partnership was consultative, candid and all designed around not only the financial viability of the project for each partner but also the overall attractiveness of the project, most importantly, to homebuyers and their guests. Conversely, there are a few local projects that didn't turn out so well, and in looking at the reasons behind any lack of success, one of the explanations is that there wasn't a good developer/manager partnership in place from the start. The early visionaries not only had good vision, but they trusted one another as well. In the same way that, as Steve Jobs pointed out, disruptions seldom come from within an industry, the developer mind and the operator mind were distinctly different. When they succeeded, it was due to the strength of their partnerships—few, if any, went it alone. That's another reason that so many of the emerging planned communities worked—it was a small town, and people just knew one another.

In addition to that dynamic, there were a small handful of families who owned larger tracts in the area who chose to develop the communities themselves—typically at a much slower rate—but in most cases, the developers bought tracts outright from the local families who had owned them for years. The dynamic around wealth creation—from tract owner, to developer, to individual homeowner—is a remarkable one that carried with it the seeds for many a debate over time and continues to this day.

Bob DeGabrielle, Pine Island and the Birth of the Luxury Rental Home

In the wake of Brindley's success in Corolla Light, the attraction of the Currituck Outer Banks as a vacation destination began to catch on more broadly in the minds of investors and builders. Other entrepreneurs, in turn, began to shape their own ideas about pushing the rental home frontier in terms of size, sophistication and even luxury. Even with the boldness of their ideas, few, if any, could have imagined the explosion of development their ideas would unleash. Important events, it turns out, can seldom be attributed to one thing, and the birth of the luxury rental home is bathed in context.

To understand this growth, we must once again look to history. Just to the south of Corolla Light, the Pine Island Hunt Club had been in existence since roughly 1913. Over time, the club expanded its real estate holdings until, in addition to its extensive soundside holdings, the Club also came to own more than six hundred acres of oceanfront land as well. The owner of the club in the '60s and '70s was a gentleman named Earl Stick, a noted entrepreneur and outdoors enthusiast from Winston-Salem, North Carolina. Stick loved the Pine Island area, and in 1979—probably with a sense of coming development—he and his family donated a large portion of the club's holdings to the Audubon Society in an effort to preserve this unique geography and natural environment from development. In a story that warrants yet another book, the Audubon Society, in a still-controversial move, sold a large portion of its oceanside holdings in order to fund the operations of its larger soundside operations. Today, those operations are remarkably well preserved in what is known as the Donal C. O'Brien Jr. National Audubon Sanctuary in Corolla.

The oceanfront real estate, however, is another story. In the late 1980s and through the 1990s, the Pine Island community was developed, built and marketed as a vacation home destination. Yet another legendary Outer Banks developer—Bob DeGabrielle—was to transform the vacation home market from the simple, relatively small and almost rustic concept of a beach cottage into something altogether complex, luxurious and downright big. Pine Island, in other words, brought forth the big vacation homes and built a luxury home frontier that defines the industry on the Outer Banks to this day.

Up until this point, vacation homes on the Outer Banks had been relatively simple—in many cases, the idea of a beach cottage was essentially a "saltbox"—simple construction, cheaply outfitted and close to the beach. It was built for sandy floors and time outdoors. Corolla Light began to change that, as did the Village experiment in Nags Head, but DeGabrielle pushed the boundary. Corolla Light homes, for example, didn't have individual pools—the community had big shared pools, as did a few others, but few homes had any private pools. The Sanderling area, just to the south of Pine Island, was built earlier and didn't have any pools either. There are a few reasons for that—lot size, zoning, utilities and Coastal Area Management Act (CAMA) setbacks among them—but in addition to that was the sentiment that oceanfront homes didn't need a pool or that, even if they did, people wouldn't be willing to pay for it.

Children in cottage window. *Outer Banks History Center.*

The Pine Island community vision boldly and controversially challenged that idea. As rental revenues began to increase and interest rates remained relatively low as compared to the Carter years, in search of bigger returns, investors started to build bigger houses that would generate still higher cash flows. Pine Island lots, developed and marketed by DeGabrielle, were bigger than comparable lots in other communities and had room for not only bigger homes but, in some cases, even pools and beach gazebos as well. These designs were a first for the region—big homes, sophisticated décor and big investments supported big rental revenue numbers and a focus on "onboard" amenities in addition to community amenities. Bigger kitchens, for example, served more people in more bedrooms. Bigger pool areas let more people enjoy the home. Not unlike Brindley, DeGabrielle had a local track record in building other, smaller-scale Currituck Beach communities following in the style of Corolla Light, but Pine Island was to be a signature development.

DeGabrielle started to design and build homes that had never before been seen on the Outer Banks—even in the private Nags Head enclaves—and these new homes came with rental rates that had never been seen before either. To that point, the biggest homes on the Outer Banks had been the private duck clubs from almost a century earlier. Some of the Nags Head homes were sizable, but nothing like Pine Island existed. DeGabrielle—a master salesman armed with a true vision—believed that, in a *Field of Dreams* moment, if people built these kinds of homes in this place, then they would indeed rent.

One oceanfront home in particular even set a few of the early property managers on their heels—some said this home design had finally gone too far and could not be rented at what was then simply a gargantuan price of $6,000 a week.

And then, in an inflection point moment for the region, the home rented. And it kept on renting. The luxury vacation home of the Outer Banks had arrived.

Other buyers and builders followed. Prices increased, both as reflections of strong national economic currents in the 1990s and increasing demand for rental homes in what was a rapidly developing and relatively exclusive community. DeGabrielle may have sensed that this only amplified a broader trend. Nationally, for example, bigger homes continued a larger trend from 1973 to 2006 in which the average new home size in America grew by 50 percent. The increasing debt required to build these bigger homes remained relatively inexpensive by historical standards. Layer those economic facts

A group of Outer Banks realtors poses for a photo in the early 1990s. *Outer Banks History Center.*

with technology improvements; the internet began to make the destination more accessible to more people. Friends told friends over new and mobile telecommunications. Service levels increased, and more jobs increased more services. Over about fifteen years, DeGabrielle essentially built out the Pine Island community and also developed a few adjacent parcels all the way down to the old guard shack location on the Dare County line. In the 1980s and 1990s, the Pine Island community had stunned the industry, going in only about twenty years from a zealously guarded private natural environment to a stunning and entirely open-to-the-public destination. People who hadn't been up the beach in a few years were simply shocked at the growth. Historically, finance is the interaction between data points and expectations, which is to say that expectations don't always keep up with reality on the ground. It was DeGabrielle's unique genius that he was able to get reality on the ground just ahead of expectations in a similar way to what Steve Jobs did with the iPhone at a larger scale.

The trend continued. A few of the property management companies that would initially service the Pine Island community would get acquired by bigger public companies that saw the activity in the region and got interested.

Road construction on the Outer Banks.
Courtesy of Twiddy & Company.

Even up in the relatively remote areas of the four-wheel-drive-only beaches of the Currituck Outer Banks, rental homes started to be built and in some cases truly test the boundaries of rental homes. Lots were much bigger there, at lower prices, and a small collection of magnificent "millionaire's row" homes came online in the late 1990s and early 2000s that remain some of the biggest and most expensive homes anywhere on the Outer Banks.

Most of this early luxury development occurred in Currituck County, as opposed to Dare, for a few important reasons—there were fewer roads, for one reason, and that meant more land to develop. Lots were bigger and cheaper than anything farther south in the more well-known areas of Nags Head. In addition, the industry was starting to develop a track record of both consistency in rental revenues (performance) and sophistication in pricing (strategy) that larger-scale investors found attractive. The new community was simply hot, the business models were working and the rush was on. It was a trend that would not turn back—forty years later, big homes continue to be built with ever-increasing levels of luxury and sophistication. That first truly big home in Pine Island is still there, anonymous in its surroundings, but at one time and one place the fact that it worked changed the destination.

Farther south in Dare County, homes and lots remained relatively smaller and less complex, and it would take a few decades—and a trend of tearing down older homes—for that tendency to change, especially in the Kill Devil Hills oceanfront area.

GROWTH IN AND AROUND HATTERAS ISLAND

With the completion of the Bonner Bridge in 1963, Hatteras Island and the National Seashore were finally linked to the larger Outer Banks and the mainland by car travel. With this new travel, the island was itself ready for greater visitor exploration, and as with the more northern stretches of

Left: A new water tank is installed at Avon on Hatteras Island in the late 1990s. *Courtesy of the Drew Wilson Outer Banks Collection.*

Below: Visitors wave from the bow of a ferry at Hatteras Inlet in the 1990s. *Courtesy of the Drew Wilson Outer Banks Collection.*

Left: Campers at Hatteras Island in early '90s. *Courtesy of the Drew Wilson Outer Banks Collection.*

Below: Excavators work on NC 12 Pea Island in 2001. *Courtesy of the Drew Wilson Outer Banks Collection.*

A Hatteras ferry dock loads. *Courtesy of the Drew Wilson Outer Banks Collection.*

the Outer Banks, it would be a handful of entrepreneurs who would guide tourism and development efforts forward. Historically, the island had been a relatively remote part of Dare County. Over time, though, the boom in Hatteras rental home construction among its scattered villages would add significantly to the overall visitor economy in the region. Today, the island consistently represents a third of the tourism dollars in the area, and infrastructure investment in the visitor economy of the island alone represents several billion dollars—a reflection, directly, of the value of the economy at the local and state level.

Interestingly, in contrast to some of the development stories of the northern Outer Banks, the story of entrepreneurship in Hatteras Island is to a larger extent the story of native families with long-standing and deep local roots, developers and businessmen, as compared to the northern Outer Banks, where many of the developers were fairly recent additions to the area. While there is a much larger cast of contributors, two local families stand out in their visions for the area.

JOHN, STEWART AND DANNY COUCH: THE VOICES OF HATTERAS

The Couch brothers knew the area cold—they all grew up on the island as the descendants of long-standing Hatteras families. Stewart got a chance to learn the tourism trade from the ground up, first at a local company called Outer Beaches and then over time, he had the opportunity to buy his own firm—the fledgling Hatteras Realty. He was, like Brindley and Oakes, a natural salesman. Under Stewart's vision, the firm grew along with development on the island. Notably, Stewart played key roles—perhaps a defining one on the Outer Banks—in his participation and leadership of not only local leadership groups but also national vacation management organizations. This was a key contribution from Stewart—in sharing what he was learning about the business in his native Hatteras Island, he was also able to shape the emerging national trade organizations as well through his best practices and leadership methods. As he did so, he reinforced the idea that the Outer Banks was indeed a national laboratory for the industry, and best practices on the Outer Banks soon become widely acknowledged across the nation. In addition, Danny was also known for building the careers of people around him—the Hatteras Island alumni network has

Commercial fishing trawlers leave Oregon Inlet headed out to sea in the 1990s. *Courtesy of the Drew Wilson Outer Banks Collection.*

over time grown to include other nationally known business leaders who all trace their leadership development to Stewart and his business efforts.

As Hatteras Island developed south of Oregon Inlet all the way to the Village area on the southern tip of the island, Stewart's vision for community development, professionalism in the industry and local community involvement were pivotal in the way Hatteras developed. To this day, in contrast to the northern Outer Banks, Hatteras Island has no incorporated towns and maintains a more informal, less commercialized vision for not only the visitor experience but resident life as well.

Stewart's brother Danny, among many things, also shared a love of Hatteras history with many beach visitors and residents and remains the unofficial historian of the island. As a reflection of this credibility and engagement on the island, he was instrumental in the establishment of the Graveyard of the Atlantic Museum in 2002. In another example of a relatively unique Outer Banks tradition in the same form as Warren Judge or Bobby Owens, Danny has also served as an elected official for many years and played an integral role in the development of Hatteras Island over time.

John Couch, in yet another Hatteras story, has been involved in the ongoing debates around public access on Hatteras Island for many years going back to the late 1970s, when the first breezes of development began to be felt by their father, Ray. In yet another example of the right kinds of balance between the preservation of the natural environment and development, John's continuing push for public beach access, among other things, has helped keep, in a real sense, Hatteras true to its roots.

THE FAMOUS MIDGETT FAMILY OF HATTERAS ISLAND

If there is a most famous name on the Outer Banks, at the local level, competition would be tight. World-class boatbuilders with last names like Tilliett, Scarborough or Davis; long-standing fishing families Daniels or Etheridge; powerful political connections ending with Basnight; and emerging business leaders like Oakes or Brindley would all compete for the honor. But for more than three centuries, the Midgett family of Hatteras Island has played prominent roles in the history of the Outer Banks in a wide variety of capacities. From Coast Guard lifesaving heroics to savvy business operators, the family remains widely recognized on and off the island. In the case of the emerging development of the island, two brothers from the Midgett family would play a contributing role.

Before the bridge to Hatteras was completed, the only reliable way to get to Hatteras, other than by boat, was to ride a simple Manteo-to-Hatteras bus line owned and operated by two famous Outer Banks brothers: Anderson and Stockton "Stocky" Midgett. The bus was well known for traversing the then sandy and muddy roads to the remote Hatteras villages and was founded just before World War II in 1938, when the brothers were only teenagers. In between the time they founded the bus line and the bridge, they were also a part of the group that advocated for the opening of the seashore in 1953. Ten years later, once the bridge was completed, the need for the bus line fell off, and the naturally entrepreneurial brothers knew that tourism on the island was about to boom as the place was discovered by an ever-growing number of visitors. As a reflection of that, the brothers then went on to found Midgett Realty in the late 1960s. Over time, the Midgett Realty operation played key development and management roles in virtually every community and subdivision on the island over time and remains, to this day, locally owned and operated by the Midgett family for over sixty years.

JOHN HARRIS, THE RETAIL GENIUS OF KITTY HAWK KITES AND THE BOOMING BUSINESS OF FLIGHT

The founder of the famous Kitty Hawk Kites, known throughout the world as teachers of hang-glided flight and outdoor recreation, started his dream in 1974 by, in his words, being laughed out of every banker's office in the area except one. Ray White, who we'll meet again later, didn't laugh out loud and actually came to see the building—the old garage of the once legendary (Louis Armstrong himself had played there in 1958) but now damaged Outer Banks Casino—where Harris wanted to start his business. Near Jockey's Ridge, the sand dune complex that is today the most visited state park in North Carolina, Kitty Hawk Kites slowly grew from its early garage to a place where, in 1986, it had the chance to build something that would put the business plainly on the map to the increasing numbers of visitors venturing forth from places like Bob Oakes's nearby community.

The connector, as John calls it, is the flagship Kitty Hawk Kites facility directly across from Jockey's Ridge. Built by John Harris and Ralph Buxton, it's a beautiful and large building, home to several affiliated Kitty Hawk Kites businesses and many others. Located right on the bypass highway, and

Kitty Hawk Kites. *Courtesy of Twiddy & Company.*

built in 1986, when interest rates started to come down significantly from the peaks in the late 1970s and when enough visitors had started arriving to raise enough eyebrows to quiet the laughter among lenders who knew they missed an opportunity, the building is now the foundation of what has become the original Outer Banks retail empire. Today, Kitty Hawk Kites has more than twenty locations across the East Coast, and John Harris is regarded by many as the dean of the Outer Banks commercial community. It was, once again, that year of 1986 that launched, in the form of Harris's vision for his company, another Outer Banks growth story. If it's true that the Outer Banks economy can best be summarized by a big *T* in the form of tourism and then three little Rs—restaurants, retail and real estate— under that umbrella, then the retail part owes much of its early dynamism to Harris. To his credit, John also shines a light on many others who have joined with him or supported Ralph and him along the way.

RETAIL FOOTPRINTS ANCHORING RESIDENTIAL DEVELOPMENT

At the same time Harris and Buxton were building their retail operations, other surprisingly sophisticated retail areas were developed as well. The Outer Banks Mall, stunning in its opening, opened close to both Harris's shop and Oakes's community in 1984. Farther north, the Marketplace commercial footprint—this one contained a grocery store in what was then a big improvement for local residents (many of whom still went to Norfolk or Elizabeth City to do bulk shopping)—began to be developed in the late 1980s. Central to the Outer Banks, the so-called Dare Centre complex came online in the early 1990s with Belk's department store anchoring the site. Walmart was to follow, in a watershed moment, in Kitty Hawk in 1992.

These sites served the increasing number of tourists to the area. As those visitors enjoyed their vacations, they spent more money on entertainment and shopping options. What stands out, with the benefit of hindsight, is that it all happened so fast. In an interesting side note, all of those locations continue to operate today.

Hotels, Motels and Running the Government: Warren and Tess Judge

Warren and Tess Judge arrived about the same time—Warren got here a little early in 1987 so Tess could keep the kids in school in Greensboro, according to Tess—and began to work in the hotel business along the beach road. Warren, over time, ran for office and shaped the local government. Tess ran the hotels and restaurants as everyone knew. Warren went on to serve for many years as a local elected official in a place that he loved. He served on the tourism board for nine years and the airport development board and was elected to the board of commissioners, where he would serve for sixteen years, with eleven years as chair—all with a background of tourism in the Nags Head and Kill Devil Hills area. In addition to their work in hotels, Warren was instrumental in the opening of the Outer Banks Hospital (the first of its kind) in 2002, among other things. He was known, above all, as someone who showed up—Warren simply was everywhere with energy.

Tess remembers those early days well:

> *I can distinctly remember that, after Labor Day, you could ride down the beach road and really not see anybody. The restaurants would all close, and the houses would get boarded up. We had to close the hotels, of course, because the labor to run them cost more than you could get for a room after the summer season was over. What's changed the most, in my mind, from those days in*

Outer Banks Hospital. *Courtesy of Twiddy & Company.*

terms of the calendar is that we see a much longer season now than we did
back then. To see the beach road so busy now in the October and Thanksgiving
time frame is something that was just unimaginable back then.

With Warren's passing, Tess stepped into a wide range of roles on the
Outer Banks—in fact, according to one close friend, the only role she doesn't
have is the one that's sitting still. Active today in a host of causes and courses,
her applied experience from the early tourism days of the 1980s to the
bustling year-round activity of today informs many would-be businessmen
and women on the right kind of journey for the region.

The Brothers White and Progress

Ray and Stan White were born and raised in Manns Harbor, just across
from Roanoke Island on the mainland side. Both are remarkable in their
contributions, public and private, and many local businesspeople credit
Ray's banking and Stan's advice for assistance along their journeys.

Ray White spent much of his Outer Banks career as a loan officer and
banker—an increasingly busy one—although he also spent a large amount
of time helping people in other ways too. Ray's ability to offer a loan helped
many an early business get off the ground, and he was also known as someone
who would take an idea seriously in a time when dreams abounded. He
was also a founding member of the Outer Banks Community Foundation,
among many other roles over a lifetime of service.

Stan White opened what would become Stan White Realty in Nags
Head in 1984 and moved into a bigger—and still current—office in
1986. Stan also served in political roles both at the local level—he was a
Board of Transportation member and former chair of the Dare County
Commissioners, among others—and the state level in the North Carolina
Senate. Stan's business advice, political connections and local touch guided
many a resident over time. John Harris, of Kitty Hawk Kites fame, credits
both of them:

Kitty Hawk Kites exists because of Ray White's belief in us. Our first
office didn't even have plumbing, for example—that existed in a small shed
out back. Think about that for a moment—Ray helped us grow out of a
garage because he saw something in us that I'm not sure we saw. I'd go

to visit Ray's office in Nags Head, and he'd have three phones on his desk and they'd literally all be ringing. When I showed up, though, he always took the time to listen to me. I can't tell you what that meant to me back then—we were just getting started, and he took the time to listen.

I always valued Stan's advice as well as Ralph, and I tried to grow the business over time. They were both always there, always kind, and treated us well—and those were the early days, remember, and I've never forgotten that.

STERLING AND JANE WEBSTER: THE OPENING OF THE RAMADA HOTEL

In 1985, along the beach road and not far from John's stores and Tess's hotels, Sterling Webster had a partnership and an idea—a collection of private condominiums along the oceanfront that could be rented out for short stays. He had great connections in nearby Hampton Roads, Virginia, and bought the land in Kill Devil Hills to build a complex. Over time, through 1985 and 1986, construction costs ran high. In thinking through building delays and rising costs, Sterling began to wonder if the idea itself would work. In order to complete the project, in 1986 Sterling and his partners applied for and received a Ramada franchise. It was a golden franchise for the Outer Banks when it opened later that year and set the tone for the future of the hotel business along the beach. Jane Webster remembers a few things from that time:

I remember that the beach road during those times was just simply deserted after Labor Day. You'd go home after five o'clock, and I mean this with no exaggeration—you wouldn't see another car on the road. Everything was closed, and there wasn't much money to eat out anyway.

In those days, if you had a hotel you had to do it all because either you couldn't find help if you could afford it or you couldn't afford help when you could find it. Sterling and I did all the jobs in a hotel over time. I'm here to tell you if you ever want an exercise and a diet routine, you just try changing hotel beds all day. It was hard work.

Years later, Sterling and Jane went on to play an important role in the development of the popular Hilton Garden Inn hotel in Kitty Hawk,

North Carolina, with other partners. Sterling never met a stranger and knew everyone in town. Both hotels are prominent in their operations and locations to this day.

Sterling has since passed, and Jane has gone on to become nothing short of a humanitarian on the Outer Banks, playing critical leadership roles in philanthropy, board governance and networking. The famous thinker Albert Schweitzer was once asked if leading by example was an important characteristic of leadership. Schweitzer disagreed—it was, he responded, the only one. If that's true, Jane fits the mold. Few are the conversations along the beach that, when a crossroads seems imminent, doesn't end with the popular refrain, "Let's just call Jane. She'll know what to do."

GEORGE CROCKER, MIKE KELLY AND THE GREAT RESTAURANTS

As the real estate industry began to truly come to life, so, too, did subsequent retail and restaurant attractions. It was this economic flywheel—jobs, disposable income, lending, more people and so forth—that made restaurant growth possible as well. The restaurant industry along the beaches boomed during the 1980s alongside the real estate and visitor economy, and one destination dining example of that boom was the opening of the soon-to-be-legendary Kelly's Restaurant in 1985. To understand that opening, we first need to meet the brilliant George Crocker.

George Crocker, like Dick Brindley, was larger than life and every bit the visionary. His retail impulse, in operating the stunning Galleon Esplanade shopping center through the 1970s and early 1980s, was ahead of its time. (The building would eventually be torn down and replaced with rental homes.) Equally, his signature next-door restaurant, A Restaurant By George, was stunning in its

Mike Kelly laughing in Kelly's Restaurant, a local establishment he founded in 1985. An Outer Banks restaurateur who spent more than fifty years in the business, Kelly understood the importance of integrating a business into the life and fabric of its surrounding community. *Outer Banks History Center.*

relative grandeur and sophistication, creating a new kind of shopping and dining experience in the area. George also had experience with hotels and was a marketing genius. Many retail operators today got their start working for Crocker.

Long before he was an Outer Banks institution, Mike Kelly helped run the restaurant with George and displayed a remarkable talent for hospitality—diners at A Restaurant By George would often comment that Crocker and Kelly simply made everyone feel famous for eating there. After Kelly bought the building for what would become Kelly's Restaurant in 1985, it soon became the capital of Outer Banks nightlife. Through the success at this restaurant, Kelly would be able to build other successful restaurants over time and help other budding restaurant entrepreneurs get their start. Wes Stepp, for example, who owns and operates several Outer Banks restaurants today, helped Kelly run the kitchen early in Kelly's career.

Rufus Pritchard, another prominent and respected businessman who for many years has owned and operated the Dunes Restaurant in Nags Head, shared this funny story about his own restaurant opening based on Mike's advice:

> At the time, I was working in banking at East Carolina Bank. I had the chance to buy a restaurant building in 1982, and the only other person I knew on the Outer Banks who had any experience in running a restaurant was Mike Kelly. So I called Mike and asked him what he thought; he repeated back to me that I didn't have any experience running a restaurant and have never worked in one, and I said that was true. He promptly told me that I should stay in banking for as long as I could. So, we opened the Dunes Restaurant in 1983, and Mike has always encouraged me.

While all the restaurant openings and closings along the beaches would warrant an entirely separate book, what stands out is that this early entrepreneurial drive included members of the real estate, retail and restaurant industries together as they all worked to create and share an Outer Banks that was a desirable destination. Remarkably, many of these businessmen and women also harbored a desire to share what they'd learned—quite a few of the leaders of the Outer Banks business community of today learned from or around these early leaders, whose visions continue to be vibrant to this very day.

COMPETITIVE LANDSCAPES THAT BUILT COMPETITIVE BUSINESS MODELS

The dreamers and business leaders who built these early sales and rental management companies are as diverse as the companies they created—many of which, as is so often the case with founders, came to reflect the personality of the founders themselves. The development of their business models alone is worthy of a case study, and for our purposes, learning how the businesses developed lends an understanding to the area's journey as a whole. In other words, these companies flowed toward commerce and reflected the demands of commerce in the eyes of the builders as they grew.

Overall, the landscape for real estate firms on the Outer Banks remains relatively fragmented, with a large number of firms in the space. Each firm has its own ownership structure and operating philosophy, and in many cases, that dynamic has evolved over time as a reflection of not only working markets but the needs of the owners as well.

EMERGING OWNERSHIP STRUCTURES AND THE BIRTH OF A NATIONAL BRAND

Different companies subsequently evolved over time. Some firms began as small family businesses—the proverbial mom-and-pops—and over time either stayed that way as they grew or took on different additional partners or business features to sustain growth. Some firms were sold to other companies and kept the branding; others sold and rebranded. Still others were acquired by public entities while others remained in private hands.

Among public brands, the success of the Outer Banks vacation rental community had by the late 1990s begun to attract the attention of hospitality brands with national aspirations; in 1998, the area's first national vacation rental brand was launched in the form of ResortQuest. The company came to life through an initial group of partnering businesses—one, called Brindley and Brindley and founded in 1985 by Dick's son Doug, from the Outer Banks—and a software designer as well. Over time, the public company grew but never gained the national brand status that its founders had set out to achieve. The company is no longer in operation, although many of its subsidiaries exist in other forms (for example, the software company was eventually purchased by Homeaway, which operates today as Vrbo). It was, in the end, a risky yet farsighted gamble but one that was ahead of its time and yet another example of the rising awareness of the vacation rental market. The next iteration of a company like this did not emerge for another twenty years.

Still other firms remained in private hands; several of the leading firms on the Outer Banks today are still owned by founding entrepreneurial families who have participated and shaped growth over decades.

Operating Philosophies as Different as the People in Them

As they grew, companies also differentiated themselves in their operations. While many firms started as specialists in a particular subdivision or community, with growth, they also developed expertise in certain areas. Some firms focused on service delivery in the form of maintenance technicians (recall Jim Braithwaite's thinking around a hiring ecosystem) or other service professionals. Others focused on creating value through marketing or outright real estate sales as core competencies. Geography played a role, too, in this diversification—some firms grew geographically within the Outer Banks with offices from the Corolla community all the way down to Hatteras and Ocracoke Islands. Others stayed relatively focused on a small number of communities in an effort to focus thematically.

Inevitably, companies also began to differentiate themselves on the approach to their homeowner communities. In other industries, this approach would be called a portfolio construction; collections of similar types of homes under a common management umbrella remain perhaps the most pronounced difference between operating companies as they grew from the '80s through the booms of the mid-2000s. Critically, the scarcest homes—oceanfront properties—historically have been the most resilient in the face of economic turbulence as a reflection of two things: (1) the scarcity of the location and (2) the cash flows that supported ever-increasing levels of luxury and complexity that underpinned the quality of the home. The higher the quality of the overall portfolio, the greater the resilience of not only the homeowner but their management and service partners as well.

Technology played an important role as well over time; with the rise of the internet and mobile communications in the bustling mid-1990s,

Proud new vacation home owners.
Courtesy of Twiddy & Company.

many local firms began to compete with various forms of performance marketing and technological innovation that informed much of the industry nationally. Specifically, website development and search engine optimization innovations that occurred on the Outer Banks led to developments across the nation in terms of guest engagement and awareness. In addition, the increasing use of technology in the early 1990s began to inform a data-driven approach to what for many years had been more of an art than a science—rental pricing that translates, in financial reality, into financial performance for investing homeowners in search of a return.

Explosive Growth
in the Service Industry as Well

As the number of rental homes grew, and as the amenities either in or around the homes grew in tandem with the complexity of the homes, the businesses providing increasing levels of services to these homes grew exponentially. Several of the largest HVAC companies of today were founded in the mid-1980s, for example, and many dominant service companies today trace their roots to the early developments. Pools and pool servicing, for example, emerged as a significant business and employer.

In fact, the key commercial trades overall—electricians, plumbers and HVAC suppliers—had a remarkable evolution on the Outer Banks during this time in part due to the nature of the region. In a market overwhelmingly dominated by short-term vacation rentals, the speed in a service response becomes increasingly important when compared to longer-term rentals. Failure to deliver a service or feature in a short-term environment, for example, can rapidly lead to refunds that turn a profitable week into a business loss. With the focus on speed in the market, strong service partners emerged with a focus on prompt and effective service responses that in practice meant vehicle fleets and on-hand inventory. The makeup of the service industry on the Outer Banks remains different than larger urban areas to this day, with the primary customer, in many cases, being someone interested in a prompt response as an alternative to a refund.

So-called last-mile challenges remain critical for bulk service providers with warehouse and logistic space competing in price with residential and commercial uses. In the mid-1980s, these challenges were not considered as important as they are nearly forty years later; there was simply more available land at the time with a terminal growth thought a long way down the road. As a result, today many of the key bulk service providers manufacture and service their products at a distance from the Outer Banks as a reflection of the costs of real estate and the size of the labor market.

3

PILLARS AND PARTNERS

Bridges to the Dreams

If you ask the right questions, there is always more to the story.
—Robert Caro

To step back a moment in our journey, we've seen a few currents emerge clearly as guiding forces in the development of the Outer Banks around the year 1986—a favorable and relatively attractive capital market that flowed from national economic and fiscal policy, a relatively affordable real estate portfolio emerging as vacation rental homes became viable business models, a collection of visionary entrepreneurs who could sense the wind and had the courage to take a risk and a few of the positive business dynamics around building a full-time employment ecosystem among the villages and towns of the Outer Banks. Nothing succeeds in a vacuum, of course, and the next stop in our journey of understanding is to comprehend a powerful political capability emerging from nearby Manteo who sought, through his efforts, to combine economic policy with economic development for the region. He would become perhaps the most important local figure in the history of the Outer Banks, even beyond the Wright brothers, because although they brought flight, it was Marc Basnight who brought all those beautiful roads.

Pirates Cove construction in Manteo, North Carolina (1992). Roanoke Properties General Partnership (the General Partnership) began developing Pirate's Cove in the late 1980s. Today, the development includes single- and multifamily residential properties, a marina and a restaurant. *Outer Banks History Center.*

THE GREAT CONNECTOR:
A POWERFUL POLITICAL WILL EMERGES

Marc Basnight was simply a phenomenon. In a place famous for storms, he was, in his own right, a political hurricane that reshaped the landscape of the region. It was, on meeting him, as if some combination of the rurally imperious Lyndon Baines Johnson and the forthrightly humble Harry S. Truman had together somehow slipped into the shoes of Senator Basnight as he began his ascent in North Carolina's General Assembly. It was an improbable rise, to be sure, as North Carolina's population dynamics continued to favor growing urban and business centers like Raleigh, Greensboro and the mighty banking hub of Charlotte. His ability, beginning with his election, to shape resource allocation and funding priorities for the betterment of the visitor economy around the Outer Banks was enormously pivotal to the rise of the region as a whole.

Born in 1947 and a native of Manteo, North Carolina, Basnight was elected to serve his northeastern region in 1984 and previously served, critically, as a member of North Carolina's Transportation Board from 1977 to 1983. (He chaired Dare County's Tourism Board prior to that.) He would go on to serve thirteen full terms in office totaling twenty-six years in elected service. Crucially for the Outer Banks region, Basnight was elected president pro tempore of the North Carolina Senate in 1993 and would serve in that powerful capacity for eighteen years until his essentially forced retirement due to illness in 2011. (He was succeeded by the state's current Senate leader, Phil Berger, from central North Carolina.) Basnight would serve as the head of a legislative body longer than anyone else in state history. Best of all, he loved his native Outer Banks and worked ferociously to support a better quality of life for its citizens and a better development of its nascent economy. Doris Kearns Goodwin once said of LBJ that to fully understand Lyndon Johnson you first had to understand the soil in the rocky Texas Hill Country, where he was from; if that's true, to fully grasp Marc Basnight, you had to fully grasp the remoteness and relative isolation of the Outer Banks.

More broadly, to fully understand Basnight's ascent to power is to understand two things: first, a shaped power dynamic in Raleigh within the Senate that coalesced political power around what's called the Senate pro tempore, or the leader of the Senate. In various political shifts over time, the pro tempore's role became the focus of significant power as decision-making

Senator Marc Basnight. *Courtesy of the Drew Wilson Outer Banks Collection.*

Jim Martin, who served as the seventieth governor of North Carolina from 1985 to 1993. *Outer Banks History Center.*

ability from other roles, like the lieutenant governor, was taken away in political shifts and reversals. As Basnight gained this pro tempore position, ascending through his previous leadership of the dominant Senate appropriations committee, he was in a place to exert direct influence over virtually any budget item within the state. Some said it was a position even more powerful than the governor, and in practice, it was hard to argue that. Second, to understand Basnight's intuitive use of power is to understand as well the state's modern political caucus system, which was emerging in North Carolina during Basnight's early rise. In short, by centralizing the caucus system, much of the ability to raise and dispense political dollars came through Basnight as well. It was his gifted ability to raise vast sums of money far out of comparison to his peers, and use it to support candidates across the state, that contributed in no small measure to his longevity in power.

In turn, the next best understanding for Basnight's exceptional power becomes one of understanding the art of raising money, and in that answer lies yet another Elizabeth City introduction—Walter R. Davis.

Walter Davis grew up relatively poor and uneducated in nearby Elizabeth City in the 1920s. He moved to Texas in 1952 and became a fortune-making leader of the oil and gas industry in and around the Permian Basin. His immense success in this industry made many things possible for Davis, including some local investments in the Southern Shores area, yet he never forgot his hometown region in his prodigious philanthropic and giveback efforts. Davis took, by many accounts, the young Basnight under his wing and introduced him to many of his business and political contacts across the state. Basnight, in turn, developed close relationships with many players in the business community and translated those relationships into a remarkable ability to raise money. It was Walter Davis who contributed, through his own remarkable reputation and business clout, to Basnight's rise as a political operator and fundraiser on par with anyone else from any corner of the state. On another coincidental note, around 1986, Davis was also a major donor to the Dean Smith Center in Chapel Hill, which opened that same year.

As Basnight's time in the General Assembly grew, so did his political capacity and willpower. In addition to fundraising characteristics, Basnight was also known as a rough-and-tumble deal maker, not above twisting an arm through the budget to get what he wanted done—in more than one accounting, Basnight's LBJ-esque ability to redirect funds to the Dare County region was legendary in Raleigh. With a distinctive Outer Banks accent, a humble background and a willingness to wield political power like few others in the history of the state, his presence and policy on a wide range of infrastructure topics supported the development of countless economic initiatives across the region—not the least of which was the ability for a great many more people to visit the Outer Banks.

Locally, on the sandy ground of the Outer Banks, Basnight made transportation—good roads and bridges—his signature priority. Many a road was improved, widened and linked to other road systems during his tenure. One prominent example of this priority was the widening of the vitally important Virginia-facing road in Currituck County leading to the Outer Banks from the interstates of Virginia, completed in 1992. The road was widened from essentially a two-lane rural road to a five-lane highway through which a majority of Outer Banks visitors would arrive on the beaches. For many years, small signs along that road after its completion said simply, "Thank you Senator Basnight."

That road improvement was followed by the Washington Baum Bridge in 1994 and the Virginia Dare Bridge in 1997, both major capital expenditures linking the Outer Banks to other population bases both in and out of the state. As an example, the fine four-lane road linking the state capital of Raleigh to the Outer Banks (much of which was improved during his tenure) was for many years known simply as Marc Basnight's Driveway.

Since his departure from elected office, the region hasn't seen anywhere near the pace of infrastructure investment. His relatively sudden departure from office left several infrastructure priorities unsettled, notably the Mid-Currituck Bridge.

While our story has focused on economic policy and development along the Outer Banks from largely the perspective of the visitor economy, Basnight was able to economically develop adjacent industries on the Outer Banks as well. For example, the Wanchese community of Roanoke Island was home to something called the Wanchese Seafood Industrial Park as an economic development project intended to support marine-based businesses. The park, established in 1981, floundered initially as a result in part of difficult dredging operations that did not allow deep-water access to

Senator Marc Basnight before accepting nomination as leader of North Carolina Senate Democrats (1992). During his tenure, Basnight became one of North Carolina's most powerful political leaders while serving a record eighteen years as Senate leader. *Outer Banks History Center.*

The more than one-mile-long Washington Baum Bridge, linking Roanoke Island with Nags Head, nears completion in 1990. It replaced a 1953 two-lane wood and concrete bridge. *Outer Banks History Center.*

Anglers fish from boats on Croatan Sound in early 1990s. *Courtesy of the Drew Wilson Outer Banks Collection.*

the facility. Basnight essentially amended the use of the facility in 1995 to allow for the usage of boatbuilding. That event supported, almost overnight, a boatbuilding industry within the park at a scale that would become, in time, a global sportfishing capital and home to many millions of dollars in annual economic impact. Those beach visitors might go fishing while they went on vacation, and the fishing industry at large remains remarkably popular (and financially reliant) on the visitor economy, although many of the park's customers are global as well.

In yet another example of Basnight's influence at the local infrastructure level, northeastern North Carolina had long been served at the community college level by the state's first community college in Elizabeth City, College of The Albemarle. Celebrating roughly twenty-five years in 1984, under Basnight's leadership, the college opened its first satellite office (the institution serves seven counties) in Manteo in 1984. Today, Manteo is home to a stellar College of The Albemarle campus focused on workforce roles in the visitor economy.

While he is enduringly known statewide for his strong support of healthcare and the university education, it is difficult to understate his impact locally in terms of transportation—in short, Basnight funded all those magnificent bridges and roads that would get all these people here to pay for the homes that Brindley, Oakes and so many others were building. As Jim Braithwaite mentioned earlier, the perception around a visitor takeoff in the 1990s was a direct reflection of a decade's worth of public infrastructure investment in the road and bridge system of the region.

Basnight's vision for a vibrant visitor economy along the Outer Banks is strongly felt today, and his infrastructure efforts are perhaps the single most important differentiator for the market as a destination overall. For example, the Outer Banks is within an easy day's drive of roughly 60 percent of the population of the United States, and it was Senator Basnight who made sure of it.

A SHIFTING EQUILIBRIUM AS BASNIGHT EXITS

Senator Basnight stepped down from his role in early 2011 for health reasons. The times were changing, too, with a newly powerful Republican Party making significant inroads in the minds of North Carolina voters. Prior to that, essentially since the conclusion of the Civil War, North Carolina, along with many other southern states, had been solidly Democratic—although that was a trend that would end across the Southeast around 2010. However, one prominent local politician remarked that, during Basnight's time in office along the Outer Banks, "you could hold a Republican meeting in a phone booth and you had better turn out the light."

Since his departure, the region has seen an unsurprisingly slow pace of infrastructure development as other parts of the state sought to catch up to Basnight's transportation focus in Eastern North Carolina. Much of the region's infrastructure today is more than twenty years old. Successive legislators have worked to carve out their own identities and priorities in the shadow of Basnight, and they have found that it's simply, in the minds of their constituents, a tough act to follow in terms of personality and temperament, one, and the ability to drive resource allocations second.

The Owens Family

The growth of the Outer Banks is in many ways the cumulative biographies of many of its citizens. Among this group of citizens, the Owens family stands out as a fine example of business, government, infrastructure and the development of tourism. Bobby Owens, the current mayor of Manteo, has been involved in politics in one way or another for most of his adult life, which is saying something, as he turns over ninety years young. Owens has played a role in the development of Dare County for many years, beginning first with his twenty-six-year run as a county commissioner, with much of that as chair, beginning in the late 1970s. In addition to that role, he's also served in a wide range of other capacities, including the North Carolina Banking Commission, the powerful North Carolina Utilities Commission and several other important roles. Among his many roles, perhaps his most enduring and yet relatively unappreciated is his pursuit, on behalf of the county, of high-quality water. While hard to imagine for the modern visitor, Dare County was not famous for most of its history for good water. It was a visit to Florida for Owens that really began a process that culminated in the construction of a reverse osmosis plant to provide continually reliable water to residents and visitors alike.

Dare County Water System construction of a five-million-gallon storage plant (1988) designed to solve Outer Banks water shortages. *Outer Banks History Center.*

The family restaurant—named, simply, after the family—remains the oldest family-owned restaurant in the same place in North Carolina, as it opened its doors in 1946. Both Bobby and his wife, Sarah, who we met earlier in our story through her connection to Outer Banks tourism, were instrumental in the rise of the Outer Banks as a destination where people could not only visit in happiness but also live in happiness.

Owens's son, R.V., is also a noted Outer Banks restaurant owner and entrepreneur who has, like his father, combined an innate business streak with a desire to serve others. Through a strong family connection to Senator Basnight—Basnight was an uncle—R.V. Owens served in a wide variety of public and fundraising roles. He continues to play an influential role today through strong political relationships and business experience.

STRENGTH AT THE STATE AND FEDERAL LEVELS AS WELL

A Historic State Partner: Governor Jim Hunt

Although Basnight's ability to shape economic policy in Eastern North Carolina was unparalleled, other important political allies participated in or supported the rise of the Outer Banks as well.

Governor Jim Hunt is the only person in North Carolina history to have

Former North Carolina governor Jim Hunt, 1990. Hunt was the sixty-ninth and seventy-first governor of North Carolina (1977–1985; 1993–2001) and is the longest-serving governor in the state's history. *Outer Banks History Center.*

been elected to four terms in the governor's mansion; his first term spanned from 1977 to 1985 and then, as an encore, once again from 1993 to 2001. He was the state's lieutenant governor from 1973 to 1977. In his time leading the state, he redefined in many ways what a modern executive role looked like in terms of gubernatorial capacity and power. As Hunt hailed from the same political party as Basnight, they supported each other in a myriad of ways—Hunt supported increasing levels of the state's gas tax, for example, that helped pay for many of Basnight's road improvements. By the year 2000, in one startling example of Hunt's legacy, it was estimated that he had appointed more than twelve thousand people to various roles in government, which, in conjunction with Basnight's appointment ability emanating from the Senate, meant that the two of them were able to influence an incredibly wide network within government across the state.

A Federal Icon as Well: Senator Jesse Helms

On the other side of the political aisle, not to mention at a different level of government, lay yet another North Carolina icon in the form of Jesse Helms. A leader of the Republican Party (both Basnight and Hunt were Democrats) and staunch conservative voice, Helms remains the longest-serving popularly elected senator in the history of North Carolina.

While relations between the three men were not always polite—Helms faced Hunt in a bitter and historically expensive race for a Senate seat after Hunt left the Governor's Office—it was a different time politically. People could disagree and still work together on important issues, and that was remarkably important for an Outer Banks region that still had critical relationships with the federal government going back to the 1930s and beyond. Lighthouses, federal claims to navigable waters (for example, the ocean inlets in and around the region), significant military populations, the National Park Service and many other issues brought the three men into conversations frequently.

With the triumvirate of Basnight at the helm of North Carolina's legislative budget, Hunt with dominant and long-standing influence at the State's executive level and Helms's seniority at the U.S. Senate level,

The dredge *Merritt* works to keep Oregon Inlet channel clear in the 1990s. *Courtesy of the Drew Wilson Outer Banks Collection.*

the Outer Banks had at the time a truly historic combination of political willpower, capacity and support. That combination remains as unique as the Outer Banks themselves.

THE INTERSECTION OF LOCAL LAND USE PLANNING AND THE STATE'S COASTAL ENVIRONMENT

In 1974, the North Carolina Legislature passed something called the Coastal Area Management Act that governed the so-called setbacks for development in sensitive coastal areas. Intended as a balance between local planning efforts—in many cases geared toward development—and statewide preservation and environment issues affecting the coastal zone of the entire state, the act has been modified in several different legislative sessions since its inception. For the purposes of the Outer Banks, the act (known more commonly as simply CAMA) introduced a permit system any time development occurs, or is planned to occur, in a defined coastal area.

Overwash occurs where the old S curves north of Rodanthe had been replaced with new pavement westward of the old road. *Courtesy of the Drew Wilson Outer Banks Collection.*

Setbacks are of key consideration to developers and property owners, of course, and over time, more favorable setbacks (to developing owners, at least) have also sparked development, particularly along the oceanfront.

In addition, in a long and relatively complicated history, the national flood insurance program gradually made homes being built in northern beaches eligible for flood insurance (much of the "paved road" sections of the Outer Banks were eligible already). It's important to note two things here: one is that eligibility is distinct from cost, as different flood zones came with different levels of perceived risk, and second that eligibility in any form transfers risk from the potential homeowner (at a cost) but that risk is protected from a total loss. In short, flood insurance eligibility supports further development along the beaches.

The Underappreciated and Critical Importance of Zoning

Over a period of remarkable growth, one component of planning that is often undervalued is the aspect of zoning. In many cases, commercial development that came online in the late 1990s or 2000s was a reflection of zoning decisions made in the 1960s or even 1970s. In explaining the growth of the area, the imaginations of the early zoning bodies are difficult to underestimate; for example, one prominent early local banker, when asked about a lack of modern local housing, replied with this honest sentiment in a public forum in 2020:

> *You have to understand, back then we just never imagined we would have this kind of growth. We had grown up with nothing, and the place was just wide open. We thought a hotel or two was a big deal back then. It's easy to look out the window today and say well we got zoning wrong, but the people who say that weren't at the meeting back then; we know we slit our own throats on affordable housing but, you have to understand, we just never could have imagined what this place has become.*

4

TOO SMALL TO FAIL

Small-Town Partnerships with Big Impacts

As the Outer Banks sparked to commercial life in the mid-1980s, that growth also carried with it the seeds of budding conservationist movements and nonprofit organizations. As with any sustained change, movements like these inevitably and correctly arise around the right balance to conserve assets as opposed to developing assets. As growth intensified, so too did the needs to protect and conserve the things that made the region unique to begin with. It is a conversation that continues very much into the present day, although many of our tools and techniques to manage change were created years ago.

During the early 1980s, local organizations began to emerge to do the things that government either wasn't able to do, didn't prioritize or didn't create value in ways that would allow the private sector to build them. As is the case in so many places, these areas and organizations tend to become at risk or even lost to pronounced growth—historic preservation, for example, or other culturally important linkages to the past. This period along the Outer Banks also fortunately contained several equally as capable, determined and visionary leaders in those fields.

Enter the Conservationist: The Physics Between Development and Conservation

Definition: Enantiodromia–*the tendency that, when given an excess of one thing, the opposite emerges.*

John Wilson was only twenty-seven years old when he was elected mayor of Manteo in 1979. A ninth-generation native of Roanoke Island, Wilson had an unparalleled vision for an Outer Banks that protected and conserved its links to the past, which led to a long series of significant contributions that continue to make the region unique in many ways. Wilson's vision of maintaining something truly singular is on display, among other places, in the Manteo of today, which has few retail or restaurant chains of any kind and a wealth of state and federal cultural resources across the island.

In addition to his public work, reported in the *New York Times*, in uniquely developing the downtown of Manteo around small businesses and protecting its historic homes, his nonprofit Outer Banks Conservationists was created in 1980 and has through the years saved countless historic or cultural resources. Wilson is a historic architect by training, and his designs are among the most widely recognized in the region. Notably, the nonprofit group protects and operates the Currituck Beach Lighthouse under an agreement with the government and also maintains and operates the Island Farm historic complex in Manteo. Wilson has, either directly or indirectly, saved hundreds of buildings across the region.

As a signature moment, during Wilson's time as mayor, Manteo played an important role in what was the United States's 400th anniversary going back to the initial Lost Colony arrival in 1587. In preparing for the events in Manteo, attended by the governor and England's Princess Anne, Wilson advocated for and shepherded more than $10 million in local state investment (a staggering amount at the time)—all with long-term tourism in mind. It was yet another example of state-level investment in infrastructure and attractions combining with local visionaries on the ground.

Wilson is no stranger to controversy, as one so active in so many different capacities is bound to generate debate. Wilson's gift, however, has been that he's been able to sense trends early and to move well before any other interested parties have been able even to muster an interest. For example, the conservationist movement to protect the soaring Currituck Lighthouse came against a backdrop of county officials at the time asking the state to burn

Former Manteo mayor John Wilson (*standing behind*) with former North Carolina governor Jim Hunt (*center*) and actor Andy Griffith (*left*). *Outer Banks History Center*.

John Wilson, mayor of Manteo in the late 1980s. *Courtesy of the Drew Wilson Outer Banks Collection*.

Actor Andy Griffith, who made his home on North Carolina's Roanoke Island, talks to former Manteo commissioner and mayor John Wilson and other local residents during the filming of a scene of *Matlock* on North Carolina's Outer Banks. *Outer Banks History Center.*

down parts of the complex as a public nuisance. Today, by comparison, the lighthouse complex alone draws hundreds of thousands of visitors a year as they visit Currituck, and Wilson's vision is directly responsible for it.

Wilson also had excellent relationships with many people across the state, from experienced state leaders like Governor Jim Hunt to star-powered local residents like Andy Griffith. Warm and considerate in person, he is also keenly aware of political power bases and the shifting dynamics of influence. Wilson's vision has kept largely intact an Outer Banks historic building community that without his persistence would most likely have vanished long ago. Wilson has, in the fullness of time, done more to protect local history than perhaps anyone else.

HELPING OTHERS: THE CREATION OF AN OUTER BANKS COMMUNITY FOUNDATION

In a remarkably quiet turn of events, 1982 also marked the creation of the Outer Banks Community Foundation—Frank Stick's son and historian

David Stick, local banker Ray White and noted entrepreneurs George Crocker and Eddie Greene were among the founders—as a charitable entity geared toward creating scholarships, grants and also emergent issues like disaster recovery. (The foundation raised more than $1 million in forty-eight hours just after Hurricane Dorian's damaging arrival in Ocracoke in 2019.) Ray White, the same banker who had believed in John Harris, was also a key member of that early team:

> *When I was younger, we didn't have a community foundation because we just didn't have enough to do that kind of thing. For example, I lived in Manns Harbor when I was a child. I caught a ferry, if you can believe that, to go to school in Manteo. We didn't have any of these bridges. It was only over time that we, as a community, began to amass the kind of wealth that would let someone be charitable and donate something so that someone else might be able to thrive. We didn't imagine what it would become today, but we knew we had a chance to do something.*

Importantly, the majority of the foundation's founders had business backgrounds, and it was those businesses that helped support the launch of the foundation. In yet another example of the value of the visitor economy's

Actor Andy Griffith, David Stick, Eddie Greene and George Crocker at an Outer Banks Community Foundation event. *Courtesy of the Drew Wilson Outer Banks Collection.*

Wright Brothers Bridge and its new replacement from Kitty Hawk to Point Harbor. *Courtesy of the Drew Wilson Outer Banks Collection.*

flywheel, the foundation has over time thrived in parallel to the business community. In 2022, the Outer Banks Community Foundation celebrated its fortieth year as a charitable local organization. Over its four decades, the foundation has supported millions of dollars in scholarships, grants and disaster recovery.

The Prototype, the First Resort Community and Saving the State's Most Visited State Park: Jockey's Ridge

The story of the turning bulldozer on the sound side of what is today Jockey's Ridge State Park is well known; Carolista Baum's work standing in front of the actual bulldozer helped spark a public awareness around the importance of the towering dune complex as a cultural and historic area. Broadly, the saving of the dune complex takes place against the backdrop of the very first resort complex on the Outer Banks. The oceanfront row of homes opposite Jockey's Ridge on the oceanside were built by seasonal residents complete with their own entertainment and amenities. As the prototype area for both development and conservation, the historic Nags Head oceanfront row and the state park at their doorsteps is a microcosm of so much that was yet to come.

But back to the bulldozer. In addition to Baum, people like the ever-present entrepreneur George Crocker and the formidable local attorney Charles Evans also helped build awareness around the dune complex in Raleigh through the construction of something called People to Preserve Jockey's Ridge. At the time, Evans was the mayor of Nags Head (a forerunner of Bob Oakes with a similar conservation approach) and would go on to serve not only in the state's General Assembly but also in a myriad of important state-level roles. While it was Carolista's work that galvanized public attention, it was also the relationships of prominent business owners and elected officials that helped shape a public and state effort around the preservation of the park that became official in 1975. A supporting nonprofit, today called Friends of Jockey's Ridge, was born in 1990 as a follow-up to the early group. Today, Jockey's Ridge is the most visited state park in North Carolina (which is remarkable given the strength of the state's park system overall).

Interestingly, it is no coincidence that the dune complex itself lies in proximity to some of the oldest private vacation homes in the state. In an area, literally across the street, known as the "Unpainted Aristocracy," early vacationers to the Outer Banks built a series of private vacation homes for family use beginning in the late 1800s. Many of the homes remain in the hands of the original families and are gorgeous reminders of early tourism on the beaches. In fact, the complex of homes—some dating to early owners from the 1850s—can make a rightful claim to be the early forerunners of Brindley and Oakes in that the home collection also had a small general store as a form of entertainment. In addition, the home complexes also were among the first oceanside homes on the Outer Banks, as many of the earliest second homes were located on the soundside as a reflection of the waterborne nature of the arrival of their guests. It was a Dr. Pool, a prominent resident from nearby Elizabeth City, who built the first oceanside home in the area in 1855 and also—in a pattern to be repeated many times in the coming years—helped secure other real estate for his friends and family. In the coming years, the neighborhood home complexes would become home to not only a general store but also a church, grocery and the famous Outer Banks Casino that brought world-class entertainment to the area for many years to come. It was in the garage of the defunct casino that John Harris, years later, would again launch a development wave across the region.

In a telling example of the importance of ongoing development and important conservation, one of the earliest resort destinations in the region lies directly adjacent to one of the Outer Banks' most important conservation projects as a poignant reminder of balance in a delicate ecosystem. It is a story replicated, in a smaller scale, all across the Outer Banks.

FINDING NEW USES FOR FORGOTTEN BUILDINGS

Among other preservation efforts, the few remaining old buildings around the Outer Banks in the 1980s came under increasing development pressure as prices and markets began to increase land prices. While many of the old structures no longer remain, a collection of a few of the most poignant Outer Banks buildings fortunately remain—the lifesaving stations.

In 1986, with development in places like Nags Head and Kill Devil Hills coming on, several old buildings began to become available for either an outright teardown to make way for a new home or some kind of preservation. That preservation, in many cases, meant a move for the building.

The Kill Devil Hills Life-Saving Station Moved to Corolla

In a particularly telling story of business growth, new markets and preserving a link to the past, local businessman Doug Twiddy purchased the original Kill Devil Hills Life-Saving Station in 1986 and moved it, piece by piece, to the tiny village of Corolla at the same time the Corolla Light community was developing. As Twiddy related the tale:

> *The station really was about to be torn down, and I had called the owners with some frequency and mentioned that if they ever wanted to part with it I would love to have it. In short, they finally called but said I had to move it. The only place where land was cheap enough to put it was in Corolla, so we cut it up into several pieces and moved it right up Duck Road. We put it back together on a lot there in the village, and we've kept it as a kind of office of some sort over all these years. It is still an original station, built in the late 1800s, and this one has direct linkages to the Wright brothers, among other things. At the time, no one on the Outer Banks—except for John Wilson—wanted to talk about historic preservation.*

The Wright Brothers Monument. *Courtesy of Twiddy & Company.*

Top: Construction takes place near Corolla Light, Currituck Beach, 1989. *Outer Banks History Center.*

Bottom: A construction worker hammers a brace into the shingled roof of a beach and tennis club built on the oceanfront of what is today the Village at Nags Head, an ocean to sound community (1988). *Outer Banks History Center.*

Twiddy and his wife, Sharon, went on to preserve the Wash Woods Coast Guard Station up in the four-wheel-drive beaches in 1992 in addition to a collection of smaller buildings in the Corolla Village area. Among the collection of buildings in the village is another old Nags Head oceanfront home moved to the area.

Tax Structures That Did Good

Both Dare and Currituck Counties—home to much of the traditional Outer Banks—had up until the 1980s been painfully remote and essentially considered more a part of the Hampton Roads, Virginia market than North Carolina. (Currituck County, for example, is considered part of the Hampton Roads Metropolitan Statistical Area.) With the emergence of Marc Basnight as a political force coupled with the nascent but exciting residential development pace of the beaches, county governments began, slowly, to take notice of development and, more importantly, the resources—and revenue—associated with a booming economy.

Marc Basnight, member of the North Carolina State Senate, representing District 1 from 1985 to 2011, registers amusement with Ken Mann, past president of the Outer Banks Chamber of Commerce (1989). *Outer Banks History Center.*

The Outer Banks have long been a favorite family vacation destination. *Courtesy of Twiddy & Company.*

What really began to affect the counties—to make them rich, really—was the surprising strength of the visitor economy as it really started to take off after Basnight's road focus in the late '80s and early '90s. Beginning in 1983, something called occupancy taxes began to open quite a few eyes to the performance of the visitor market. In short, over time, these lodging taxes (paid in addition to state and local sales taxes) have directly generated billions of dollars and indirectly supported many billions more in visitor spending. How local governments would spend this money became a story all its own, and because the money stays local by state law, how the counties would spend the money became a key regional differentiator over time. In other words, as local businesses began to thrive, so did the local counties via tax collections. (For example, Dare County has an appointed tourism authority that allocates resources, while in neighboring Currituck, the elected officials themselves are the tourism authority.) Dare and Currituck, notably, consistently remain in the top tier

Linemen work to move a power line on Hatteras Island back away from the ocean in early 1990s. *Courtesy of the Drew Wilson Outer Banks Collection.*

of overall county occupancy tax collections across the state, comparing favorably with much larger destinations like Raleigh or Charlotte. As yet another example of Basnight's continuing influence, out of one hundred total counties in North Carolina, only seven are by law allowed to collect an additional local excise tax on the sale of real estate—the seven counties, perhaps to no surprise, match closely with Basnight's Senate district.

These counties in turn invest much of these dollars into marketing and infrastructure projects that support not only better quality of life for full-time residents but also longer-term tourism experiences. By doing so, the public sector counties support the private sector businesses that generate the taxes. Over time, that symbiotic relationship has driven much of the Outer Banks visitors and residents see today. To highlight the partnership, Doug Twiddy puts it this way:

> *One important thing to remember was the availability of utilities. For a long time, the water in Duck was simply terrible, and homes were serviced only by private wells. Over time, public water came along, and that really helped. As they ran water further and further up the road, you got to see that good subdivisions followed good utilities.*

A Concurrent Mandate for Education Around the Natural Environment

Business vibrancy, along with the political will of people like Marc Basnight and Bobby Owens, also helped sow the early seeds of what has become a surprisingly varied vibrant natural environment education setting.

Beginning in 1976 with the initial North Carolina Marine Resource Center in Manteo, the system was renamed the Aquariums in 1986 in a gesture toward public engagement.

In an initial federal commitment to research, the Duck Research Pier, established on federal property just to the north of the community of Duck, was established in 1977 with a mission to develop coastal research to be used across the United States.

Five years later, in 1982, the North Carolina Coastal Federation was established to share extensive research and engagement around so-called living shorelines as both commercial and residential development continued along the waterfront areas of the Outer Banks. The federation

Anglers crowd a fishing pier in the 1990s. *Courtesy of the Drew Wilson Outer Banks Collection.*

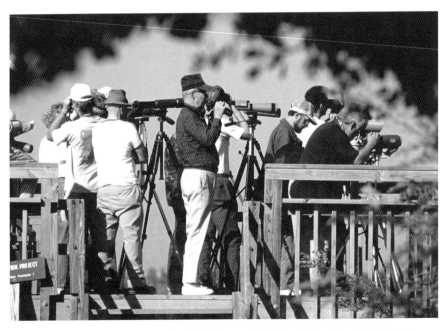

Bird watchers at Pea Island in the late '80s. *Courtesy of the Drew Wilson Outer Banks Collection.*

also helps support education and research with oyster habitats and marine resource planning.

The Coastal Studies Institute, another Marc Basnight project, was established on Roanoke Island in 2003 as a collaborative research environment to be shared among educational institutions.

The famous Jennette's Pier, initially built in Nags Head in 1939, was reimagined (once again under Basnight's leadership) in 2011 as a popular extension of the North Carolina Aquarium footprint on Roanoke Island. In addition to its recreation offerings, it highlights an extensive education mission focused on the coastal aquatic habitat. It remains a major tourist attraction.

THE SET STAGE

This combination so far has been the rising action of the drama—larger-than-life personalities, against-the-odds risk takers, changing economic landscapes, a desolate adversity overcome and the cheering applause of welcome rural infrastructure all via key moments along the way. Of course, with hindsight being 20/20, we know these outcomes all led to the initial booms of tourism in the late 1980s through the '90s. Now, we turn our focus from the doers and their efforts to their legacies.

5

THE JOURNEY SINCE 1986

Après the initial sparks of residential vacation home development around 1986, the Outer Banks as we know it today began to emerge clearly. With Corolla coming on the map with its surprisingly grand resort, Duck emerging as a viable commercial village and Nags Head beginning to see master planned vacation home communities, the model would be set for others to follow. Other subdivisions began to be imagined— in many cases, aware of the newfound value of their real estate holdings, families sold large tracts to developers, or in fewer cases, those same families chose to develop the land themselves. For example, in a further connection with Elizabeth City, the Small family decided to develop a section just north of Duck called Carolina Dunes just a bit at a time and maintained family ownership for many years in doing so. That approach is in contrast to many other subdivisions, but the Carolina Dunes approach worked for the family over the long term. In just about every case, the subdivisions were built to be vacation homes owned as second or investment homes by people living off the island. Many of them, taking a cue from the success of Brindley and Oakes, included the amenities that kept people coming back and also created real jobs for local residents. The popular Four Seasons community of Duck, for example, began to grow in the early 2000s and was envisioned from the ground up with the kind of amenities—pools and open spaces— that had made Corolla Light such a hit. Once the initial development dominoes of Corolla and Nags Head began to move, others were quick to follow, and in rapid succession, much of the northern Outer Banks began to see development interest.

Aerial of Corolla, North Carolina beach. *Courtesy of Twiddy & Company.*

With the stock market crash of 1987 and the savings-and-loan implosion at roughly the same time, though, capital markets weakened by comparison—with rising inflation numbers of late 1986, the Federal Reserve acted quickly to raise interest rates to head off another round of Carter-era economic mire. From October 1986 to October 1987, the Fed raised rates in a series of moves from 5.8 percent to 7.2 percent. Mortgage rates subsequently increased as well, heading north of 10 percent and not receding below that number again until 1991 under President George H.W. Bush. The rate reversal marked the end of the longest peacetime economic expansion in U.S. history, and the resulting recession of 1990 and 1991 was mild by historic comparison. Although, once again, George H.W. Bush was to be a one-term president in part because of a sense of economic underperformance.

By extension, locally, construction slowed down as well, although it still continued because some investors, stung by losses in the traditional stock markets, began to believe that owning and operating a vacation home wasn't a bad financial investment. People, despite the economic headwinds of various market cycles, still came on vacation, meaning cash flows remained consistent—a notion made clear in the late '80s and that still holds true today. Quite a few rental homeowners today count their real estate investment as a key piece of their overall portfolio and rely on their rental homes to sustain consistent cash flows over time. If there is one specific reason for the growth of the vacation home market overall, it is this—they perform well in and out of market cycles, and people just keep coming.

The next time mortgage rates began to drop—this would be toward the sunset of the George H.W. Bush presidency—Marc Basnight was heading the powerful Appropriations Committee in the North Carolina Senate and was able to appropriate funding for a range of road and bridge projects locally. Once those projects were completed and mortgage rates began to drop, the Outer Banks again saw a burst of interest in buying and building but also, for the first time, visitation at a scale meaning enough people to pack out the few restaurants open through the summer. In fact, many of the restaurants marking the landscape of the Outer Banks were built in the mid-1990s. It was those roads and bridges that made it possible. Crucially, all those diners had places to stay, and they were enjoying themselves. Better still, they employed a lot of people in getting ready for them, and their sales taxes paid for things that the local communities simply never had.

It's important to note this equilibrium shift. While the 1980s were when the risk-takers began to sense their timing was right, tourism as we know it today didn't really occur until the 1990s—a fact that's borne out by the various visitation numbers from the time. With the recession of the early 1990s in the rearview mirror, the mid-'90s saw more economic growth that supported stronger tourism levels across the nation. The year 1993, in that perhaps ultimate economic bellwether, saw Walmart open on the Outer Banks as the rising visitor economy began to attract national retail attention. The following year, 1994, under the presidency of Bill Clinton, saw lower post-recession interest rates triggering a strong year for economic growth across the country. Under a Clinton administration, the country would see a remarkable period of growth that Clinton summarized in his 2000 State of the Union Address:

> *We begin the new century with over twenty million new jobs; the fastest economic growth in more than thirty years; the lowest unemployment rates in thirty years; the lowest poverty rates in twenty years; the lowest African American and Hispanic unemployment rates on record; the first back-to-back surpluses in forty-two years; and next month, America will achieve the longest period of economic growth in our entire history. We have built a new economy.*

To be specific, the so-called prime rate in 1990 was a solid 10 percent; only four years later, in 1994, it had decreased to 6.1 percent. In 1995, it slowed down a bit, as the Fed once again raised rates quickly to avoid the potential for slowing growth. (Greenspan described, in early 1996, the economic numbers as "dismal.") In hindsight, between 1993 and 2000, the United States exhibited the best financial performance in more than four decades. Notably, innovations related to the internet and communications technology and productivity rose as well.

In short, the United States saw a ten-year annual increase in gross domestic product that didn't subside until around the "dot-com" bubble in 2001, although that year is largely overshadowed in our minds by the horror of 9/11. In effect, that period of economic stability supported rising tides of disposable income that helped visitors arrive on the Outer Banks over those beautiful roads and stay in all those beautiful new homes.

GROWTH CONTINUES THROUGH 2005

The Outer Banks continued to grow on a relatively smooth trend line through the 1990s, with increasing tourism driving up prices for vacation stays, which in turn fueled greater demand for construction and development. After the recession, housing markets and interest rates had returned to 1980's patterns, and low energy prices contributed to a willingness for much of the American public to take a vacation by car.

In 2001, in an effort to head off economic declines—notably after 9/11—the Federal Reserve lowered interest rates significantly. This trend, linked to increasing homeownership targets and also in search of economic resilience after the national tragedy, continued right up until 2005 and yet another round of interest rate increases. But by then, it was too late to head off the bursting of the bubble.

That growth chapter culminated in a real housing boom up until 2005—one that, in the words of Howard Marks, carried the seeds of its own failure within its success. For context, in 2001 under a George W. Bush presidency, the Fed began to aggressively lower interest rates. In 2003 (the same time as the Four Seasons community of Duck took off), Fannie and Freddie May bought more than $81 billion in subprime mortgages—a move that incentivized increasing home loans by loosening regulations and federalizing risk. Broadly, in 2004, U.S. homeownership peaked at an all-time high of 69 percent.

On the Outer Banks, the combination of looser credit regulations and low interest rates had the intended effect. Homes continued to be built at a rapid pace (again, the gorgeous Four Season community in Duck was started in late 2000 and saw a burst of construction in the mid-2000s). All those new homes, of course, contributed to what was by now a boom in visitation as well. As the Outer Banks began to become more popular, all these new visitors needed a place to stay. As home prices rapidly increased, however, complicated rules around capital structures allowed for risky lending, and in short, the inevitable correction along the Outer Banks was both not surprising in its cyclical arrival but stunning in its severity based on recent memories. When, over the course of 2004 to 2006, the Federal Reserve raised rates in seventeen consecutive quarterly meetings, that meant that floating mortgages got a lot more expensive. As they did so, the problem, like a fire, burst out of the bag.

The Problem That No One Saw Coming: The 2007–8 Housing Bubble

The well-documented housing crisis in the United States touched off a financial firestorm globally known as the Great Recession and, in effect, cooled significantly the housing trends on the Outer Banks for several years. While home prices fluctuated drastically, another interesting inflection point emerged once again: people, despite the recession, still came on vacation, and they stayed in all of these new homes that had their sale prices moving all around. That meant that rental revenues to homeowners stayed relatively intact, and it was that trend that staved off large-scale economic destruction to the rental home community on the Outer Banks. To be sure, there was meaningful investor damage, but that didn't lead to any larger, more systemic failures in the local economy. In the fullness of time, despite the financial damage, one conclusion that grew brighter was that these rental homes were consistent as economic engines across market cycles. In other words, despite the national drama, the Outer Banks visitor economy was reliable in a time of remarkable uncertainty in many other financial markets.

Despite the bubble, this home construction trend meant that there were quite a few new and relatively high-end vacation homes to be managed, operated and serviced for homeowners and their guests. Property management companies grew, service partners launched and hired and the full-time population grew considerably during this time.

The 2020 COVID Pandemic, the Bridge Closure and the Roar Back

The popularity of the region continued to grow in the wake of the housing crisis although at a slower pace as buying and selling remained slower than the boom years leading up to 2007. It would take yet another national event to once again change the course of the Outer Banks.

The first inklings of what would become the global COVID pandemic began to arrive in February 2020, and in an unprecedented step, the Dare County commissioners made the drastic and emotional decision in March 2020 to close Marc Basnight's magnificent bridge accesses to the Outer Banks for all nonresidents, homeowner and guest alike. The highly controversial and nationally unique decision was made under the auspices of a lack of healthcare availability on the Outer Banks to support a widespread contagion but also carried extraordinary risk to the singularly dominant visitor economy that either directly or indirectly supported the region.

The transition from one era to another occasionally occurs on an exact date—the Victorian era, for example, probably ended on an exact date in World War I, during the First Battle of the Somme. The age of flight, as another example, began on December 17, 1903. For the Outer Banks visitor economy, there is perhaps no other defining date that captures a boom more so than the bridge reopening of May 2020. There was no particular reason for that date as an opening, other than perhaps the grudging realization that the elected leaders had erred about as far as they could go and now were becoming increasingly vulnerable to large-scale nonresident lawsuits and the vast economic destruction of their own constituents. In truth, without the stunning amounts of federal assistance to businesses, the Outer Banks economy could have been recast as a result of the decision. That said, recriminations were short-lived. While no one could have ever predicted a man-made decision to close the bridges, no one in turn could have predicted what would happen when they opened again.

As the pandemic wrought havoc across the United States, the vacation rental industry began to emerge nationally as a bright spot in an otherwise disastrous travel and tourism landscape. Large companies like Airbnb (founded in 2008) and Vrbo (founded in 1995) had created a growing national awareness for home rentals as an alternative to hotel lodging. That niche reflected exceptionally well on the Outer Banks, which features a relatively large selection of single-family homes as a segment of the overall lodging market.

As the bridge reopened, the reputation of the Outer Banks as a family destination combined with complex perceptions of relative safety caused demand for rental homes in the area to simply explode. In effect, any company or organization operating in the visitor economy saw record revenues in 2020, 2021 and 2022. By extension, local governments did as well through subsequent tax collections. While a large percentage of those guests had visited the Outer Banks before, a significant number were also new to the region, visiting because their traditional first-choice vacations, such as international flights, theme destinations or contained entertainment like cruises, was simply unavailable to them. (For example, the world's most visited theme park, Walt Disney World, closed on March 12, 2020, for several months.)

The years 2021 and 2022 saw a continuation of that demand, with the ongoing pandemic and an increasing number of repeat visitors as more people began to discover and enjoy the destination. As a result, yet another real estate market boom occurred, with home prices significantly increasing in a short period of time—partly because of the increase in rental revenues and partly because of the perception of desirability as an alternative investment. As of this writing in 2023, this boom has yet to subside, and the popularity of the Outer Banks is bringing forth new challenges for the future.

WHAT HAS EMERGED FROM ALL THIS?

It has been almost forty years since the initial flames of the now booming visitor economy were lit around 1986. The remarkable entertainment destination of the Outer Banks has become famous in quite a few ways—popular television shows (Aycock Brown would have loved them), charming Nicholas Sparks novels and excellent marketing campaigns from both public and private entities keep the Outer Banks in the very forefront of vacation awareness in the United States. In any relatively short period of time that sees change to this extent, there remains some combination of happiness with the benefits that the industry has brought to the beaches mixed with some real sense of loss—quite a few Outer Banks lovers, for example, can still clearly remember what it was like before things got quite so popular.

In trying to contextualize the change, it's worth pausing for a moment to consider what all those early entrepreneurs really brought forth in terms of lasting effects and influence.

First and foremost, the Outer Banks has emerged clearly as America's Seashore. In a place so close to the major population centers around our nation's capital and as a shining example of the power of public access, as Roosevelt envisioned it, the Outer Banks stands as a unique, popular destination in America. That it wasn't lost amid chain development, or dangerous hurricanes, or through a lack of planning remains a key distinction—local planning has, for the most part, been exceptional although it has seemed painstakingly slow or occasionally misguided in the moment. By and large, the destination—especially when compared to other competing destinations across the Southeast—has remained largely intact in its beauty. One measure of success for those early risk-takers would be in defining the right balance between building the right things and not building the wrong things—or, in the words of the poet, the fear of losing what they had while not getting what they wanted. In that measure, they were remarkably successful.

Second, the entrepreneurial drive of the founding businessmen and women remains. As a destination, the Outer Banks is notable in one aspect for its remarkably high percentage of vacation homes as a reflection of the overall pool of lodging options—by some measures, the Outer Banks

A Nags Head house damaged after Hurricane Emily in 1993. *Courtesy of the Drew Wilson Outer Banks Collection.*

Top: An aerial view of oceanfront homes along North Carolina's Outer Banks. *Courtesy of Twiddy & Company.*

Bottom: Sunset in Kill Devil Hills, North Carolina. *Courtesy of Twiddy & Company.*

Top: Pelicans resting on the beach. *Courtesy of Twiddy & Company.*

Bottom: Sunrise at the pier. *Courtesy of Twiddy & Company.*

competes with only the Orlando area in the sheer size and variability of the vacation home market. Within this large catalog of vacation home options remains another key to the long-term vibrancy of its vacation homes—the industry remains remarkably competitive with more than twenty major firms competing for market share, service delivery and visitor loyalty. This competition has brought significant value to homeowners and visitors over time—keeping prices relatively low, services at the very forefront of the industry nationally and commercial tourism technology at state-of-the-art

Visitors enjoying the beaches of the Outer Banks. *Outer Banks History Center.*

levels as well. Firms simply cannot get complacent, especially as newer national organizations compete alongside the long-standing family firms that started around 1986.

For some context, residential real estate in the United States is by some measures a more than $1 trillion asset class. In considering the sheer size of that real estate market, it's indeed remarkable to consider that the Outer Banks has emerged as a capital of what is now a major asset class in America—residential operating real estate. By that measure, the early entrepreneurs created a business model that many others in the nation watch as an example and by doing so set a national standard for the industry. They are, in many a judgment, best in class, and what they were doing was among the best in America.

Third, the importance of infrastructure stands out for not only current capacity but future capability as well. Basnight's ability to build an infrastructure for the present as well as the future vacationer speaks to his strategic gift and, in parallel, his ability to build a consensus around economic development as economic policy. Said differently, he was the rare political thinker who was able to proactively build the future while at the same time enhancing the present. Whether it is education, healthcare, utility infrastructure or all those simply beautiful roads, his vision was ahead of his time, and we are all better off for it. It has been said that great trees are planted so that one day, people we will never meet will sit in the shade under them. In that definition, Basnight was a remarkable visionary.

Finally, the gifts and grit of those early business builders endure as an example. The most powerful teachers are inevitably those who set the most powerful examples, and the 1986 generation remains a potent example of big ideas, big risks and the American dream. Their most important contribution, if measured in the place today, lies ironically not in their creations but in their ability to inspire others to follow in their footsteps, as millions upon millions have indeed done. The Outer Banks is a great place, full of unique businesses, operated by new generations who studied the earlier generation or, in many a case, learned at their feet. The place and their example simply endure.

CONCLUSION

Progress requires both optimism and pessimism to co-exist.
—Morgan Housel

Today, North Carolina's tourism economy is a more than $30 billion annual industry with the lodging sector making up more than $6 billion of that directly. Dare and Currituck Counties, despite their relatively low population, rank consistently among the state's largest tourism drivers, competing well with much larger counties like Wake (Raleigh) or Mecklenburg (Charlotte). Vacation rentals, through the pandemic, led the recovery in many ways of the larger tourism industry across the state. Nowhere was that recovery more pronounced than on the Outer Banks, where the vibrancy of the area continues to amaze and astonish those remaining early entrepreneurs.

With demographic trends in major urban centers continuing to grow, the demand for vacations on the Outer Banks has continued to increase in proportion to regional population growth. With Basnight's visionary transportation networks making access to the Outer Banks faster than many other destinations, the fundamentals of the Outer Banks' success continue to look favorable—a beautiful place, easy to get to, close to a lot of people and still unique.

Challenges remain, of course, although they change over time. Going back to 1986, one of the best aspects of the Outer Banks was sheer affordability. While that remains true on a relative basis compared to many other coastal destinations, housing is today a critical challenge, especially for working families. At the national level, housing is broadly in a state of crisis as well; much of America simply stopped building in the wake of the Great Recession of the 2008 range. Population numbers continued to increase, however, and nationally some measures put our housing deficit at a stunning level of four or five million homes short to meet the national demand.

Along the Outer Banks, a place with limited land footprints, housing challenges are as unique as the place. Ironically, as all these new rental homes continued to be built, and as the destination flourished, one unintended outcome was that to the investor, the attractiveness of short-term occupancy revenues outpaced the attractiveness of long-term occupancy revenues. Said more clearly, weekly rental homes make more money than longer-term rentals, and that fact has put enormous pressure on the long-term housing market in the form of drastically increased rental rates. Broadly speaking, short-term money is made in real estate through cash flows and cash flows multiples—and both of those measures favor shorter-term rentals (particularly in a time of rising demand, as short-stay rates can be flexible as demand rises). That reality has made, especially since the bridge reopening of 2020, housing for working families in the region challenging at best—median home prices, in fact, have seen healthy double-digit growth in each of the past three consecutive years. With changing demographics around an aging population and an increasing demand for services along the region's shores, the worrisome combination of a decline in working housing alongside a shrinking labor pool is worthy of the best strategic minds. In the long term, the only thing the islands cannot afford to lose are the bright working professionals in the hospitality industry who do so much for so many. Hope for the future of working housing lies most likely in a regional approach to housing, although increasing commute times anger some residents, who feel displaced through the rising economy. The Outer Banks is not alone in this journey, as other populations—Hawaii, for example, or the Lake Tahoe area—are contending with similar challenges. In order for the Outer Banks to remain as it is, though, housing is going to have to become available at a quality and proximity that keeps it attractive to working families. It would be a remarkable irony indeed if, at some point in the future, it was the service providers—the successors of the one-time locals—who came to need the bridge to get to the visitors who live along the shore in a place once inhabited, not that long ago, by only the locals.

It is this trend that may define the next group of visionaries as well; perhaps the deepest attraction to a sense of vision from the past is the tantalizing question of who, among us, may burst forth next in their audacity. As the Outer Banks grows, many of its challenges may indeed outgrow the small patch of sand nestled in and among the bridges—as Aycock Brown foresaw so many years ago, the Outer Banks is much more of a cohesive region than any particular town or place. The answer to our modern challenges, as we look toward the future, may lie in growing once again as Brown and the early entrepreneurs did so well. Elizabeth City, for example, the home of some of the first vacation builders and public opinion influencers, may very well be among the next regions to associate with the Outer Banks not only as part of the brand but as part of the infrastructure and housing footprint as well. Dr. Pool's house, for example, the same Dr. Pool who perhaps built the first oceanfront vacation home in the mid-1800s in Nags Head, still stands prominently downtown and may very well await an entrepreneur. It would be a unique return to the beginning.

In other words, to grow the Outer Banks and sustain the work that has built the beaches, the next group of visionaries may well have to once again develop the destination beyond what was once considered only a narrow sandbar. As Brindley did in Corolla, or Braithwaite in Duck, so, too, may the next generation proceed in terms of building in places where there was once very little idea of what could be. We eagerly await the boldness of their ideas and their grit in seeing through an increasingly regional destination. The fundamental entrepreneurial key, based on what we have learned since 1986, may rest in the notion that to solve our problems and build the future we must have the courage to grow beyond the boundaries of today.

Politically, one changing aspect since the departure of Senator Basnight is the mandate for locally elected state officials to work in unison at the regional level—where Basnight had the political ability to drive resource allocation virtually on his own, the population dynamics of today suggest that only through regional and collaborative cohesion will state-level resources and infrastructure once again flow to the area as it grows. It may very well be that political vision, in addition to private sector vision, is a foundational part of the regional growth fabric for years to come.

Even more broadly than housing or infrastructure is an overall sense of affordability that quickly leaps into other critical industries—education, for example, as teachers are affected by relatively high costs of living. Healthcare as well is affected, as medical providers deal with acute staffing shortages that expensive housing markets do little to overcome.

As of this writing, the national economic landscape offers an interesting comparison to where our story began in some ways with the slow economy of Jimmy Carter. Interest rates, market lending and housing prices are all cooling in preparation for the next inevitable market cycle along the Outer Banks. Home prices will continue to reflect the rents that visitors are willing to pay to stay in them, and despite economic headwinds, there are many more millions of people within a tank of gas drive to the Outer Banks with not much corresponding growth in the existing home footprint. In short, while real estate cycles continue to work, the overall trend of the Outer Banks has, for more than five decades now, been an "up and to the right" optimism no matter the federal reserve environment. That's not to say caution doesn't have a rightful place, however—the scar tissue and financial trauma of the housing crisis of 2008 still remind business operators of the potential for rapid turbulence in the market. In an analogy to our foreign policy as a nation, one noted columnist once observed that the United States always seemed to prepare for the last war and never the next one. Applied more locally, that sentiment seems to suggest that the next cycle—with all its surprises—won't be like the last one and that our well-trained sense of pattern recognition will have to rely, in some measure, on an entrepreneurial imagination in order to fully position the destination to be resilient for the next challenge.

In the long term, though, there is the inevitable question of the boundaries of future development—new businesses, new buildings, new dreamers and new opportunities each built on a limited sand dune. At some unknown point, the real destination danger lies in crossing some kind of invisible line that, upon its crossing, becomes irretrievable in its departure—the place will possibly have lost what it was. The challenge of that line, of course, lies in its visibility only to historians and never the day-to-day practitioners. Hope lies, once again, in the idea that our dreamers, like the earlier generation, love the place and what it is so that they can share it with those who will come to join them out of the same love.

Embedded within any historical context, for the thoughtful reader, is inevitably a sense of imagination in search of something to learn, or a pattern to be recognized in a future setting, or perhaps even something to be replicated. In this story, one enduring refrain that stands out from several different perspectives is the notion that while the early builders knew they were onto something, the Outer Banks as it stands today was still too shrouded in the future to be clear in their minds. Time and again, in conversations for this book, a popular refrain among the longtime business leaders was, "I could not have imagined…" as mounting traffic, ongoing construction and an ever-lengthening visitor season boom along the beach.

Two questions emerge from those Wild West entrepreneurial dreamers of the mid-1980s—First, is there a formula or some kind of systemic thinking that would make that kind of vision repeatable? Second, will we see that kind of birth again with our own eyes in our own lifetimes?

Enduringly, infrastructure remains important—without it, nothing could have been built or sustained once it had. Access to capital helped, too, although times have changed now with the internet and globalization making access to capital a global, in addition to local, business. In the end, though, was the human willingness to take a risk in pursuit of a dream. As long as there are those kinds of people, there is indeed something to be learned, a pattern to be nourished and something to be built on.

What stands in counterintuitive relief, after having journeyed through the story, is that the future was unknown even to those with the strongest visions. History will repeat itself, as it always does, but curiously not in the way we expect—certainly not for us in the same way that it didn't for the beach pioneers. But amid the work, and the risks, the worry and the daunting unlikeliness of it all, it sure was fun, in a lot of ways and in a stunningly beautiful place, where the wonders of nature lie only just beyond your eyes, ears and hands. That the place is still largely intact—not swept aside, like so many other sandscaped places—is a testament not only to their vision but also their legacy for the people around them who saw their work and in turn fired dreams of their own. After all, the fact that the next business boom will be new and original is, to the true entrepreneur, reason alone and reason enough.

In the end, and as with all things, we return to where we started. A good story is, ultimately, a group of people in action as they overcome the challenges and vestiges that would keep them from achieving their potential together. A similar personality to the early Outer Banks builders and a cousin of the early Outer Banks proponent Franklin Roosevelt, Theodore Roosevelt departed his own presidential office in 1909 only six years after Wilbur and Orville had flung their contraption into the air around Kitty Hawk. This other Roosevelt gave a speech the following year that would become famous as the "man in the arena" moment. In part, it read:

> *It is not the critic who counts; not the man who points out how the strong man stumbles, or where the doer of deeds could have done them better. The credit belongs to the man who is actually in the arena, whose face is marred by dust and sweat and blood; who strives valiantly; who errs, who comes short again and again, because there is no effort without error*

Raymond Berry of Outer Banks Contractors, US 158, 1990. *Outer Banks History Center.*

A trawler leaves Oregon Inlet as the channel is dredged in the early 1990s. *Courtesy of the Drew Wilson Outer Banks Collection.*

Norris Austin, Corolla postmaster, at the old schoolhouse in the early '90s. *Courtesy of the Drew Wilson Outer Banks Collection.*

and shortcoming; but who does actually strive to do the deeds; who knows great enthusiasms, the great devotions; who spends himself in a worthy cause; who at the best knows in the end the triumph of high achievement, and who at the worst, if he fails, at least fails while daring greatly, so that his place shall never be with those cold and timid souls who neither know victory nor defeat.

His description is in many ways applicable to those early visionary entrepreneurs and builders who shaped a booming economy around our first national seashore. Many of the early shapers have since passed on, and the remaining developers are all into their seventies and eighties. The beach they built has turned over many times since their early dreams, and yet the energy of their ambition remains. The modern inheritors of their efforts, fortunately, have been guided not only by the quality of their dreams but also by the audacity of their belief. In their example, they remain fully in the place they loved.

EPILOGUE

Marc Basnight passed away in 2020 after a long battle with what is commonly known as Lou Gehrig's disease. The new bridge connecting the northern Outer Banks to Hatteras Island is named after him, and so is the North Carolina Cancer Hospital, the state's flagship cancer facility. Both honors are entirely fitting for the great man who did so much to bring the Outer Banks to the world.

Dick Brindley passed away, aged ninety, in 2018. He was a gentleman gifted with a sense of humor, a drive to succeed and an imagination that few possessed. A celebration of his life was, appropriately, held in the Corolla Chapel, only steps away from the community that in his vision set a standard for all the others.

Bob DeGabrielle, a true entrepreneur, went on to further success by starting a firm in the emerging legal cannabis industry in Colorado that would go on to become one of the largest cannabis producers in the United States.

Bob Oakes remains involved in a wide array of Outer Banks activities, including a longtime leadership role at his beloved Village Realty.

Stewart Couch, a local legend and well known throughout the national vacation industry, passed away unexpectedly in 2012. His influence, directly and indirectly, remains as vibrant as the Hatteras Island he loved.

John Wilson continues to remain the master of visionary preservation, with a link to the past few can equal in their imaginations. He is a gift to anyone who loves the Outer Banks.

Developer Bob DeGabrielle and Ret Travers stand in front of a new vacation home in the Monteray Shores, DeGabrielle's first major development (1988). *Outer Banks History Center.*

Many of the early visionaries have passed over the last decade as well; Warren Judge, Sterling Webster, Eddie Greene and the irrepressible George Crocker have all left meaningful and lasting contributions to the place we—among so many millions of others—love to this very day.

Perhaps the postscript, at a personal level, is simply this: these imaginative people, in their boom times and place, were incentivized to solve problems for a range of reasons they all understood in their own light. That they did so is their testament.

ABOUT THE AUTHOR

Clark Twiddy is the president of Twiddy & Company, a hospitality and asset management firm founded in 1978 along the Outer Banks. He was raised in Duck, North Carolina, and is a U.S. Navy veteran in addition to having served in many public, private and nonprofit roles.

He currently serves on the Towne Bank Board of Directors in addition to the Vidant Health Foundation. He is an alumnus of the Virginia Military Institute, the University of Tennessee and Northwestern's Kellogg School of Management.

Married to a native Texan, he is the father of two young daughters, and in his spare time enjoys the guitar, time on the water and the dusty memories of old houses. This is his second book about the Outer Banks.

Visit us at
www.historypress.com